A

William & Dorothy Wordsworth

A Miscellany

Introduction and selection
by Gavin Herbertson

Rucksack Editions

Galileo Publishers, Cambridge

Published by Galileo Publishers
16 Woodlands Road, Great Shelford,
Cambridge, UK, CB22 5LW

www.galileopublishing.co.uk

Galileo Publishers is an imprint of
Galileo Multimedia Ltd.

ISBN 978-1-903385-59-3

Text design by James Shurmer

Cover design by NamdesignUK

Cover illustration by Francis Towne

Rucksack Editions are based on an original concept by
Erlend Clouston

Printed in Lithuania

Also in the same series:

John Muir: A Miscellany edited by Laurie Battle
Edward Thomas: A Miscellany edited by Anna Stenning

Contents

Dorothy Wordsworth

William Wordsworth *page* 235

Poetry (*continued*):

Introduction by Gavin Herbertson

With the sun high in the sky, at the dawn of a new century, a young poet strolled along the shores of a vast lake. In quiet contemplation, his eyes washed over the horizon, meandering along the curves of the water. With a weary head, he lay his limbs down on the bank, anticipating the onset of a gentle slumber. All of a sudden, out of nowhere, he was struck by the most beautiful sight he had yet beheld. Mustering his racing mind, he scrambled for his pencil, scrawling, in barely legible verse, the most famous lines in the English language:

> I wandered lonely as a cloud
> That floats on high o'er vales and hills,
> When all at once I saw a crowd,
> A host, of golden daffodils

This is perhaps how we imagine William Wordsworth, the poet of solitary walks and rustic bliss. It was, in no small way, the image which he also projected of himself. And yet, in reality, things were very different. For one thing, when he composed 'Daffodils', he was sitting at home. For another, over two years had passed since he had seen them. Although the poem was certainly inspired by a real-life stroll through Ullswater, there was nothing solitary about its composition. Like most clouds, William did not wander alone.

As was their habit, on a 'threatening misty morning' in April 1802, William and his sister Dorothy accompanied one another on a walk. A keen diarist, she would go on to record the day's events in her journal. For any modern reader of her prose, one passage in particular stands out:

I never saw daffodils so beautiful they grew among the mossy stones about and about them, some rested their heads upon these stones as on a pillow for weariness and the rest tossed and reeled and danced and seemed as if they verily laughed with the wind that blew upon them over the lake, they looked so gay ever glancing ever changing.

Given the chronology, we know that Dorothy did not write her account after reading her brother's poem. Instead, it is very likely that, when composing his most famous lines, William had just reread his sister's description.

Born in Cockermouth on April 7th 1770, William was around a year older than his sister, and the second of their parent's five children. The two spent much of their early childhood together, but were separated in 1778 when Dorothy was sent to live with relatives in Halifax. Despite their fondness for one another, the two would remain apart for the vast majority of the next nine years. In 1795, Wordsworth met Samuel Taylor Coleridge, his lifelong friend, and co-author of the *Lyrical Ballads* (1798). The collection would kick-start the so-called "Romantic" strain in English poetry, having been composed at Alfoxton House, in Somerset, where Dorothy also wrote the first of her major journals. One of the most significant collections of poetry in any language, the major works of the *Lyrical Ballads* – from 'Michael' to 'Tintern Abbey' – have been included in this volume.

In the latter poem, William alludes to the importance of Dorothy directly, terming her a 'dear, dear Friend', in whom he may behold what he 'once was'. Critics are divided as to whether this representation of Dorothy is favourable, because William turns to her, or patriarchal, since he does not let her speak. Nevertheless, in either case, her great importance for the poem is recognised. To return the favour, over thirty years later, in one of her twenty seven extant poems (entitled 'Thoughts on my sick-bed'), Dorothy went on to laud the great ability of her 'Friend from infancy'. Long considered an important textual-biographical source for William's life and work, the stand-alone merit of Dorothy's writing, and the reciprocal influence of the siblings' work on each other, is beginning to be recognised. In truth, that this has been overlooked is relatively surprising since, right at the beginning of her *Grasmere Journal* (1800–1803), in which we find the daffodils anecdote, Dorothy made explicitly clear that she hoped to 'give William pleasure' by writing it.

In this collection, to highlight the interconnectedness of the two authors' work, Dorothy's most compelling narrative – 'Recollections of a Tour Made in Scotland' – bisects William's verse, having been placed immediately before 'Stepping Westward', the first of the poems which William composed on their shared journey. For the sake of narrative completion, only two sections have been omitted from the journal. A short section has been removed from the end of the second week, and the text relating to events after the fourth week has been cut, since it was composed much later, and is not as detailed in its description. William's verse has been selected according to its appropriateness as an accompaniment for a country ramble, or a leisurely hike through the hills. Poems depicting nature have been preferred over those concerned with contemporary politics, while the *Prelude* has not been included, owing to regrettable limitations of space. The collection has been ordered chronologically, according to date of composition, rather than publication. And, since William substantially revised many of his poems throughout his life, in all cases, the last versions he produced have been printed. Only the prose taken from the *Guide Through the District of the Lakes* appears out of sequence: the anonymous first version having appeared in 1810, with the fifth, fully revised edition published twenty-five years later. Since the introductory material has been reprinted, it is only fitting to place it at the beginning of the book.

It is my hope that the present volume will provide an overview of William's verse and prose, having been sourced from all stages of his diverse and storied career. At the same time, by reprinting the work alongside that of his sister, the collaborative process of their composition should be made clear. Whether the verse is self-aggrandising, and guilty of what Keats pejoratively termed Wordsworth's "egotistical sublime", remains up for debate. But, in terms of composition, there is no doubt that solitude and egoism were far from the driving forces. Overall, in a very real sense, I hope this book will provide a sibling's comfort during long country walks.

William Wordsworth

From "Description of the Scenery of the Lakes" in
A Guide Through the District of the Lakes

Section First: View of the Country as Formed by Nature

At Lucerne, in Switzerland, is shewn a Model of the Alpine country which encompasses the Lake of the four Cantons. The Spectator ascends a little platform, and sees mountains, lakes, glaciers, rivers, woods, waterfalls, and vallies, with their cottages, and every other object contained in them, lying at his feet; all things being represented in their appropriate colours. It may be easily conceived that this exhibition affords an exquisite delight to the imagination, tempting it to wander at will from valley to valley, from mountain to mountain, through the deepest recesses of the Alps. But it supplies also a more substantial pleasure: for the sublime and beautiful region, with all its hidden treasures, and their bearings and relations to each other, is thereby comprehended and understood at once.

Something of this kind, without touching upon minute details and individualities which would only confuse and embarrass, will here be attempted, in respect to the Lakes in the north of England, and the vales and mountains enclosing and surrounding them. The delineation, if tolerably executed, will, in some instances, communicate to the traveller, who has already seen the objects, new information; and will assist in giving to his recollections a more orderly arrangement than his own opportunities of observing may have permitted him to make; while it will be still more useful to the future traveller, by directing his attention at once to distinctions in things which, without such previous aid, a length of time only could enable him to discover. It is hoped, also, that this Essay may become generally serviceable, by leading to habits of more exact and considerate observation than, as far as the writer knows, have hitherto been applied to local scenery.

To begin, then, with the main outlines of the country;—I know not how to give the reader a distinct image of these more readily, than by requesting him to place himself with me, in imagination, upon some given point; let it be the top of either of the mountains, Great Gavel, or Scawfell; or, rather, let us suppose our station to be a cloud hanging midway between those two mountains, at not more than half a mile's distance from the summit of each, and not many yards above their highest elevation; we shall then see stretched at our feet a number of vallies, not fewer than eight, diverging from the point, on which we are supposed to stand, like spokes from the nave of a wheel. First, we note, lying to the south-east, the vale of Langdale, which will conduct the eye to the long lake of Winandermere, stretched nearly to the sea; or rather to the sands of the vast bay of Morcamb, serving here for the rim of this imaginary wheel;—let us trace it in a direction from the south-east towards the south, and we shall next fix our eyes upon the vale of Coniston, running up likewise from the sea, but not (as all the other vallies do) to the nave of the wheel, and therefore it may be not inaptly represented as a broken spoke sticking in the rim. Looking forth again, with an inclination towards the west, we see immediately at our feet the vale of Duddon, in which is no lake, but a copious stream winding among fields, rocks, and mountains, and terminating its course in the sands of Duddon. The fourth vale, next to be observed, viz. that of the Esk, is of the same general character as the last, yet beautifully discriminated from it by peculiar features. Its stream passes under the woody steep upon which stands Muncaster Castle, the ancient seat of the Penningtons, and after forming a short and narrow estuary enters the sea below the small town of Ravenglass. Next, almost due west, look down into, and along the deep valley of Wastdale, with its little chapel and half a dozen neat dwellings scattered upon a plain of meadow and corn-ground intersected with stone walls apparently innumerable, like a large piece of lawless patch-work, or an array of mathematical figures, such as in the ancient schools of geometry might have been sportively and fantastically traced out upon sand. Beyond this little fertile plain lies, within a bed of steep mountains, the long, narrow, stern, and desolate lake of Wastdale; and, beyond this, a dusky tract of level ground conducts the eye to the Irish Sea. The stream that issues from Wast-water is named the Irt, and falls into the estuary of the river Esk. Next comes in view Ennerdale, with its lake of bold and some-what savage shores. Its stream, the Ehen or Enna, flowing through a soft and fertile country, passes the town of Egremont, and the ruins of the castle,—then, seeming, like the other rivers, to break through the barrier of sand thrown up by the winds on this tempestuous coast, enters the Irish Sea. The vale of Buttermere, with the lake and village of that name, and Crummock-water, beyond, next present themselves. We will follow the main stream, the Coker, through the fertile and beautiful vale of Lorton, till it is lost in the Derwent, below the noble ruins of Cockermouth Castle. Lastly, Borrowdale, of which the vale of Keswick is only a continuation, stretching due north, brings us to a point nearly opposite to the vale of Winandermere with which we began. From this it will appear, that the image of a wheel, thus far exact, is little more than one half complete; but the deficiency on the eastern side may be supplied by the vales of Wytheburn, Ulswater, Hawswater, and the vale of Grasmere and Rydal; none of these, however, run up to the central point between Great Gavel and Scawfell. From this, hitherto our central point, take a flight of not more than four or five miles eastward to the ridge of Helvellyn, and you will look down upon Wytheburn and St. John's Vale, which are a branch of the vale of Keswick; upon Ulswater, stretching due east:—and not far beyond to the south-east (though from this point not visible) lie the vale and lake of Hawswater; and lastly, the vale of Grasmere, Rydal, and Ambleside, brings you back to Winandermere, thus completing, though on the eastern side in a somewhat irregular manner, the representative figure of the wheel.

Such, concisely given, is the general topographical view of the country of the Lakes in the north of England; and it may be observed, that, from the circumference to the centre, that is, from the sea or plain country to the mountain stations specified, there is—in the several ridges that enclose these vales, and divide them from each other, I mean in the forms and surfaces, first of the swelling grounds, next of the hills and rocks, and lastly of the mountains—an ascent of almost regular gradation, from elegance and richness, to their highest point of grandeur and sublimity. It follows therefore from this, first, that these rocks, hills, and mountains, must present themselves to view in stages rising above each other, the mountains clustering together towards the central point; and next, that an observer familiar with the several vales, must, from their various position in relation to the sun, have had before his eyes every possible embellishment of beauty, dignity, and splendour, which light and shadow can bestow upon objects so diversified. For example, in the vale of Winandermere, if the spectator looks for gentle and lovely scenes, his eye is turned towards the south; if for the grand, towards the north: in the vale of Keswick, which (as hath been said) lies almost due north of this, it is directly the reverse. Hence, when the sun is setting in summer far to the north-west, it is seen, by the spectator from the shores or breast of Winandermere, resting among the summits of the loftiest mountains, some of which will perhaps be half or wholly hidden by clouds, or by the blaze of light which the orb diffuses around it; and the surface of the lake will reflect before the eye correspondent colours through every variety of beauty, and through all degrees of splendour. In the vale of Keswick, at the same period, the sun sets over the humbler regions of the landscape, and showers down upon them the radiance which at once veils and glorifies,— sending forth, meanwhile, broad streams of rosy, crimson, purple, or golden light, towards the grand mountains in the south and south-east, which, thus illuminated, with all their projections and cavities, and with an intermixture of solemn shadows, are seen distinctly through a cool and clear atmosphere. Of course, there is as marked a difference between the noontide appearance of these two opposite vales. The bedimming haze that overspreads the south, and the clear atmosphere and determined shadows of the clouds in the north, at the same time of the day, are each seen in these several vales, with a contrast as striking. The reader will easily conceive in what degree the intermediate vales partake of a kindred variety.

I do not indeed know any tract of country in which, within so narrow a compass, may be found an equal variety in the influences of light and shadow upon the sublime or beautiful features of landscape; and it is owing to the combined circumstances to which the reader's attention has been directed. From a point between Great Gavel and Scawfell, a shepherd would not require more than an hour to descend into any one of eight of the principal vales by which he would be surrounded; and all the others lie (with the exception of Hawswater) at but a small distance. Yet, though clustered together, every valley has its distinct and separate character: in some instances, as if they had been formed in studied contrast to each other, and in others with the united pleasing differences and resemblances of a sisterly rivalship. This concentration of interest gives to the country a decided superiority over the most attractive districts of Scotland and Wales, especially for the pedestrian traveller. In Scotland and Wales are found, undoubtedly, individual scenes, which, in their several kinds, cannot be excelled. But, in Scotland, particularly, what long tracts of desolate country intervene! so that the traveller, when he reaches a spot deservedly of great celebrity, would find it difficult to determine how much of his pleasure is owing to excellence inherent in the landscape itself; and how much to an instantaneous recovery from an oppression left upon his spirits by the barrenness and desolation through which he has passed.

But to proceed with our survey;—and, first, of the

MOUNTAINS. Their forms are endlessly diversified, sweeping easily or boldly in simple majesty, abrupt and precipitous, or soft and elegant. In magnitude and grandeur they are individually inferior to the most celebrated of those in some other parts of this island; but, in the combinations which they make, towering above each other, or lifting themselves in ridges like the waves of a tumultuous sea, and in the beauty and variety of their surfaces and colours, they are surpassed by none.

The general surface of the mountains is turf, rendered rich and green by the moisture of the climate. Sometimes the turf, as in the neighbourhood of Newlands, is little broken, the whole covering being soft and downy pasturage. In other places rocks predominate; the soil is laid bare by torrents and burstings of water from the sides of the mountains in heavy rains; and not unfrequently their perpendicular sides are seamed by ravines (formed also by rains and torrents) which, meeting in angular points, entrench and scar the surface with numerous figures like the letters W. and Y.

In the ridge that divides Eskdale from Wasdale, granite is found; but the MOUNTAINS are for the most part composed of the stone by mineralogists termed schist, which, as you approach the plain country, gives place to limestone and free-stone; but schist being the substance of the mountains, the predominant color of their rockyparts is bluish, or hoary grey—the general tint of the lichens with which the bare stone is encrusted. With this blue or grey colour is frequently intermixed a red tinge, proceeding from the iron that interveins the stone, and impregnates the soil. The iron is the principle of decomposition in these rocks; and hence, when they become pulverized, the elementary particles crumbling down, overspread in many places the steep and almost precipitous sides of the mountains with an intermixture of colours, like the compound hues of a dove's neck. When in the heat of advancing summer, the fresh green tint of the herbage has somewhat faded, it is again revived by the appearance of the fern profusely spread over the same ground: and, upon this plant, more than upon any thing else, do the changes which the seasons make in the colouring of the mountains depend. About the first week in October, the rich green, which prevailed through the whole summer, is usually passed away. The brilliant and various colours of the fern are then in harmony with the autumnal woods; bright yellow or lemon colour, at the base of the mountains, melting gradually, through orange, to a dark russet brown towards the summits, where the plant, being more exposed to the weather, is in a more advanced state of decay. Neither heath nor furze are generally found upon the sides of these mountains, though in many places they are adorned by those plants, so beautiful when in flower. We may add, that the mountains are of height sufficient to have the surface towards the summit softened by distance, and to imbibe the finest aerial hues. In common also with other mountains, their apparent forms and colours are perpetually changed by the clouds and vapours which float round them: the effect indeed of mist or haze, in a country of this character, is like that of magic. I have seen six or seven ridges rising above each other, all created in a moment by the vapours upon the side of a mountain, which, in its ordinary appearance, shewed not a projecting point to furnish even a hint for such an operation.

I will take this opportunity of observing, that they who have studied the appearances of nature feel that the superiority, in point of visual interest, of mountainous over other countries—is more strikingly displayed in winter than in summer. This, as must be obvious, is partly owing to the forms of the mountains, which, of course, are not affected by the seasons; but also, in no small degree, to the greater variety that exists in their winter than their summer colouring. This variety is such, and so harmoniously preserved, that it leaves little cause of regret when the splendour of autumn is passed away. The oak-coppices, upon the sides of the mountains, retain russet leaves; the birch stands conspicuous with its silver stem and puce-coloured twigs; the hollies, with green leaves and scarlet berries, have come forth to view from among the deciduous trees, whose summer foliage had concealed them: the ivy is now plentifully apparent upon the stems and boughs of the trees, and upon the steep rocks. In place of the deep summer-green of the herbage and fern, many rich colours play into each other over the surface of the mountains; turf (the tints of which are interchangeably tawny-green, olive, and brown,) beds of withered fern, and grey rocks, being harmoniously blended together. The mosses and lichens are never so fresh and flourishing as in winter, if it be not a season of frost; and their minute beauties prodigally adorn the foreground. Wherever we turn, we find these productions of nature, to which winter is rather favourable than unkindly, scattered over the walls, banks of earth, rocks, and stones, and upon the trunks of trees, with the intermixture of several species of small fern, now green and fresh; and, to the observing passenger, their forms and colours are a source of inexhaustable admiration. Add to this the hoar-frost and snow, with all the varieties they create, and which volumes would not be sufficient to describe. I will content myself with one instance of the colouring produced by snow, which may not be uninteresting to painters. It is extracted from the memorandum-book of a friend; and for its accuracy I can speak, having been an eye-witness of the appearance. "I observed," says he, "the beautiful effect of the drifted snow upon the mountains, and the perfect tone of colour. From the top of the mountains downwards a rich olive was produced by the powdery snow and the grass, which olive was warmed with a little brown, and in this way harmoniously combined, by insensible gradations, with the white. The drifting took away the monotony of snow; and the whole vale of Grasmere, seen from the terrace walk in Easedale, was as varied, perhaps more so, than even in the pomp of autumn. In the distance was Loughrigg-Fell, the basin-wall of the lake: this, from the summit downward, was a rich orange-olive; then the lake of a bright olive-green, nearly the same tint as the snow-powdered mountain tops and high slopes in Easedale; and lastly, the church, with its firs, forming the centre of the view. Next to the church came nine distinguishable hills, six of them with woody sides turned towards us, all of them oak-copses with their bright red leaves and snow-powdered twigs; these hills—so variously situated in relation to each other, and to the view in general, so variously powdered, some only enough to give the herbage a rich brown tint, one intensely white and lighting up all the others—were yet so placed, as in the most inobtrusive manner to harmonise by contrast with a perfect naked, snowless bleak summit in the far distance."

Having spoken of the forms, surface, and colour of the mountains, let us descend into the VALES. Though these have been represented under the general image of the spokes of a wheel, they are, for the most part, winding; the windings of many being abrupt and intricate. And, it may be observed, that, in one circumstance, the general shape of them all has been determined by that primitive conformation through which so many became receptacles of lakes. For they are not formed, as are most of the celebrated

Welsh vallies, by an approximation of the sloping bases of the opposite mountains towards each other, leaving little more between than a channel for the passage of a hasty river; but the bottom of these vallies is mostly a spacious and gently declining area, apparently level as the floor of a temple, or the surface of a lake, and broken in many cases, by rocks and hills, which rise up like islands from the plain. In such of the vallies as make many windings, these level areas open upon the traveller in succession, divided from each other sometimes by a mutual approximation of the hills, leaving only passage for a river, sometimes by correspondent windings, without such approximation; and sometimes by a bold advance, of one mountain towards that which is opposite it. It may here be observed with propriety that the several rocks and hills, which have been described as rising up like islands from the level area of the vale, have regulated the choice of the inhabitants in the situation of their dwellings. Where none of these are found, and the inclination of the ground is not sufficiently rapid easily to carry off the waters, (as in the higher part of Langdale, for instance,) the houses are not sprinkled over the middle of the vales, but confined to their sides, being placed merely so far up the mountain as to be protected from the floods. But where these rocks and hills have been scattered over the plain of the vale, (as in Grasmere, Donnerdale, Eskdale, &.) the beauty which they give to the scene is much heightened by a single cottage, or cluster of cottages, that will be almost always found under them, or upon their sides; dryness and shelter having tempted the Dalesmen to fix their habitations there.

I shall now speak of the LAKES of this country. The form of the lake is most perfect when, like Derwent-water, and some of the smaller lakes, it least resembles that of a river; —I mean, when being looked at from any given point where the whole may be seen at once, the width of it bears such proportion to the length, that, however the outline may be diversified by far-receding bays, it never assumes the shape of a river, and is contemplated with that placid and quiet feeling which belongs peculiarly to the lake—as a body of still water under the influence of no current; reflecting therefore the clouds, the light, and all the imagery of the sky and surrounding hills; expressing also and making visible the changes of the atmosphere, and motions of the lightest breeze, and subject to agitation only from the winds—

> The visible scene
> Would enter unawares into his mind
> With all its solemn imagery, its rocks,
> Its woods, and that uncertain heaven received
> Into the bosom of the steady lake!

It must be noticed, as a favourable characteristic of the lakes of this country, that, though several of the largest, such as Winandermere, Ulswater, Haweswater, do, when the whole length of them is commanded from an elevated point, lose somewhat of the peculiar form of the lake, and assume the resemblance of a magnificent river; yet, as their shape is winding, (particularly that of Ulswater and Hawswater) when the view of the whole is obstructed by those barriers which determine the windings, and the spectator is confined to one reach, the appropriate feeling is revived; and one lake may thus in succession present to the eye the essential characteristic of many. But, though the forms of the large lakes have this advantage, it is nevertheless favourable to the beauty of the country that the largest of them are comparatively small; and that the same vale generally furnishes a succession of lakes, instead of being filled with one. The vales in North Wales, as hath been observed, are not formed for the reception of lakes; those of Switzerland, Scotland, and this part of the North of England, are so formed; but, in Switzerland and Scotland, the proportion of diffused water is often too great, as at the lake of Geneva for instance, and in most of the Scotch lakes. No doubt it sounds magnificent and flatters the imagination, to hear at a distance of expanses of water so many leagues in length and miles in width; and such ample room may be delightful to the fresh-water sailor, scudding with a lively breeze amid the rapidly-shifting scenery. But, who ever travelled along the banks of Loch-Lomond, variegated as the lower part is by islands, without feeling that a speedier termination of the long vista of blank water would be acceptable; and without wishing for an interposition of green meadows, trees, and cottages, and a sparkling stream to run by his side? In fact, a notion, of grandeur, as connected with magnitude, has seduced persons of taste into a general mistake upon this subject. It is much more desirable, for the purposes of pleasure, that lakes should be numerous, and small or middlesized, than large, not only for communication by walks and rides, but for variety, and for recurrence of similar appearances. To illustrate this by one instance:—how pleasing is it to have a ready and frequent opportunity of watching, at the outlet of a lake, the stream pushing its way among the rocks in lively contrast with the stillness from which it has escaped; and how amusing to compare its noisy and turbulent motions with the gentle playfulness of the breezes, that may be starting up or wandering here and there over the faintly-rippled surface of the broad water! I may add, as a general remark, that, in lakes of great width, the shores cannot be distinctly seen at the same time, and therefore contribute little to mutual illustration and ornament; and, if the opposite shores are out of sight of each other, like those of the American and Asiatic lakes, then unfortunately the traveller is reminded of a nobler object; he has the blankness of a sea-prospect without the grandeur and accompanying sense of power.

As the comparatively small size of the lakes in the North of England is favourable to the production of variegated landscape, their boundary-line also is for the most part gracefully or boldly indented. That uniformity which prevails in the primitive frame of the lower grounds among all chains or clusters of mountains where large bodies of still water are bedded, is broken by the secondary agents of nature, ever at work to supply the deficiences of the mould in which things were originally cast. Using the word deficiences, I do not speak with reference to those stronger emotions which a region of mountains is peculiarly fitted to excite. The bases of those huge barriers may run for a long space in straight lines, and these parallel to each other; the opposite sides of a profound vale may ascend as exact counterparts, or in mutual reflection, like the billows of a troubled sea; and the impression be, from its very simplicity, more awful and sublime. Sublimity is the result of Nature's first great dealings with the superficies of the earth; but the general tendency of her subsequent operations is towards the production of beauty; by a multiplicity of symmetrical parts uniting in a consistent whole. This is every where exemplified along the margins of these lakes. Masses of rock, that have been precipitated from the heights into the area of waters, lie in some places like stranded ships; or have acquired the compact structure of jutting piers; or project in little peninsulas crested with native wood. The smallest rivulet—one whose silent influx is scarcely noticeable in a season of dry weather—so faint is the dimple made by it on the surface of the smooth lake—will be found to have been not useless in shaping, by its deposits of gravel and soil in time of flood, a curve that would not otherwise have existed. But the more powerful brooks, encroaching upon the level of the lake, have, in course of time, given birth to ample promontories of sweeping outline that contrast boldly with the longitudinal base of the steeps on the opposite shore; while their flat or gently sloping surfaces never fail to introduce, into the midst of desolation and barrenness, the elements of fertility, even where the habitations of men may not have been raised. These alluvial promontories, however, threaten, in some places, to bisect the waters which they have long adorned; and, in course of ages, they will cause some of the lakes to dwindle into numerous and insignificant pools; which, in their turn, will finally be filled up. But, checking these intrusive calculations, let us rather be content with appearances as they are, and pursue in imagination the meandering shores, whether rugged steeps, admitting of no cultivation, descend into the water; or gently-sloping lawns and woods, or flat and fertile meadows stretch between the margin of the lake and the mountains. Among minuter recommendations will be noticed, especially along bays exposed to the setting-in of strong-winds, the curved rim of fine blue gravel, thrown up in course of time by the waves, half of it perhaps gleaming from under the water, and the corresponding half of a lighter hue; and in other parts bordering the lake, groves, if I may so call them, of reeds and bulrushes; or plots of water-lilies lifting up their large target-shaped leaves to the breeze, while the white flower is heaving upon the wave.

To these may naturally be added the birds that enliven the waters. Wild-ducks in springtime hatch their young in the islands, and upon reedy shores;—the sand-piper, flitting along the stony margins, by its restless note attracts the eye to motions as restless:—upon some jutting rock, or

at the edge of a smooth meadow, the stately heron may be
descried with folded wings, that might seem to have caught
their delicate hue from the blue waters, by the side of which
she watches for her sustenance. In winter, the lakes are
sometimes resorted to by wild swans; and in that season
habitually by widgeons, goldings, and other aquatic fowl
of the smaller species. Let me be allowed the aid of verse
to describe the evolutions which these visitants sometimes
perform, on a fine day towards the close of winter.

> Mark how the feather'd tenants of the flood,
> With grace of motion that might scarcely seem
> Inferior to angelical, prolong
> Their curious pastime! shaping in mid air
> (And sometimes with ambitious wing that soars
> High as the level of the mountain tops,)
> A circuit ampler than the lake beneath,
> Their own domain;—but ever, while intent
> On tracing and retracing that large round,
> Their jubilant activity evolves
> Hundreds of curves and circlets, to and fro,
> Upward and downward, progress intricate
> Yet unperplex'd, as if one spirit swayed
> Their indefatigable flight.—'Tis done—
> Ten times, or more, I fancied it had ceased;
> But lo! the vanish'd company again
> Ascending;—they approach—I hear their wings
> Faint, faint, at first, and then an eager sound
> Past in a moment—and as faint again!
> They tempt the sun to sport amid their plumes;
> They tempt the water or the gleaming ice,
> To shew them a fair image;—'tis themselves,
> Their own fair forms, upon the glimmering plain,
> Painted more soft and fair as they descend

Almost to touch;—then up again aloft,
Up with a sally and a flash of speed,
As if they scorn'd both resting-place and rest!

The ISLANDS, dispersed among these lakes, are neither so numerous nor so beautiful as might be expected from the account that has been given of the manner in which the level areas of the vales are so frequently diversified by rocks, hills, and hillocks, scattered over them; nor are they ornamented (as are several of the lakes in Scotland and Ireland) by the remains of castles or other places of defence; nor with the still more interesting ruins of religious edifices. Every one must regret that scarcely a vestige is left of the Oratory, consecrated to the Virgin, which stood upon Chapel-Holm in Windermere, and that the Chauntry has disappeared, where mass used to be sung, upon St. Herbert's Island, Derwent-water. The islands of the last mentioned lake are neither fortunately placed nor of pleasing shape; but if the wood upon them were managed with more taste, they might become interesting features in the landscape. There is a beautiful cluster on Winandermere; a pair pleasingly contrasted upon Rydal; nor must the solitary green island of Grasmere be forgotten. In the bosom of each of the lakes of Ennerdale and Devockwater is a single rock, which, owing to its neighbourhood to the sea, is—

"The haunt of cormorants and sea-mews' clang,"

a music well suited to the stern and wild character of the several scenes! It may be worth while here to mention (not as an object of beauty, but of curiosity) that there occasionally appears above the surface of Derwentwater, and always in the same place, a considerable tract of spongy ground covered with aquatic plants, which is called the Floating, but with more propriety might be named the

Buoyant, Island; and, on one of the pools near the lake of Esthwaite, may sometimes be seen a mossy Islet, with trees upon it, shifting about before the wind, a *lusus naturae* frequent on the great rivers of America, and not unknown in other parts of the world.

> "fas habeas invisere Tiburis arva,
> Albuneaeque lacum, atque umbras terrasque
> natantes."

This part of the subject may be concluded with observing—that, from the multitude of brooks and torrents that fall into these lakes, and of internal springs by which they are fed, and which circulate through them like veins, they are truly living lakes, "vivi lacus;" and are thus discriminated from the stagnant and sullen pools frequent among mountains that have been formed by volcanoes, and from the shallow meres found in flat and fenny countries. The water is also of crystalline purity; so that, if it were not for the reflections of the incumbent mountains by which it is darkened, a delusion might be felt, by a person resting quietly in a boat on the bosom of Winandermere or Derwent-water, similar to that which Carver so beautifully describes when he was floating alone in the middle of lake Erie or Ontario, and could almost have imagined that his boat was suspended in an element as pure as air, or rather that the air and water were one.

Having spoken of Lakes I must not omit to mention, as a kindred feature of this country, those bodies of still water called TARNS. In the economy of nature these are useful, as auxiliars to Lakes; for if the whole quantity of water which falls upon the mountains in time of storm were poured down upon the plains without intervention, in some quarters, of such receptacles, the habitable grounds would be much more subject than they are to inundation.

But, as some of the collateral brooks spend their fury, finding a free course toward and also down the channel of the main stream of the vale before those that have to pass through the higher tarns and lakes have filled their several basins, a gradual distribution is effected; and the waters thus reserved, instead of uniting, to spread ravage and deformity, with those which meet with no such detention, contribute to support, for a length of time, the vigour of many streams without a fresh fall of rain. Tarns are found in some of the vales, and are numerous upon the mountains. A Tarn, in a Vale, implies, for the most part, that the bed of the vale is not happily formed; that the water of the brooks can neither wholly escape, nor diffuse itself over a large area. Accordingly, in such situations, Tarns are often surrounded by an unsightly tract of boggy ground; but this is not always the case, and in the cultivated parts of the country, when the shores of the Tarn are determined, it differs only from the Lake in being smaller, and in belonging mostly to a smaller valley, or circular recess. Of this class of miniature lakes, Loughrigg Tarn, near Grasmere, is the most beautiful example. It has a margin of green firm meadows, of rocks, and rocky woods, a few reeds here, a little company of water-lilies there, with beds of gravel or stone beyond; a tiny stream issuing neither briskly nor sluggishly out of it; but its feeding rills, from the shortness of their course, so small as to be scarcely visible. Five or six cottages are reflected in its peaceful bosom; rocky and barren steeps rise up above the hanging enclosures; and the solemn pikes of Langdale overlook, from a distance, the low cultivated ridge of land that forms the northern boundary of this small, quiet, and fertile domain. The mountain Tarns can only be recommended to the notice of the inquisitive traveller who has time to spare. They are difficult of access and naked; yet some of them are, in their permanent forms, very grand; and there are accidents of things which would make the meanest of them interesting. At all events, one of these pools is an acceptable sight to the mountain wanderer; not merely as an incident that diversifies the prospect, but as forming in his mind a centre or conspicuous point to which objects, otherwise disconnected or insubordinated, may be referred. Some few have a varied outline, with bold heath-clad promontories; and, as they mostly lie at the foot of a steep precipice, the water where the sun is not shining upon it, appears black and sullen; and, round the margin, huge stones and masses of rock are scattered; some defying conjecture as to the means by which they came thither; and others obviously fallen from on high—the contribution of ages! A not unpleasing sadness is induced by this perplexity, and these images of decay; while the prospect of a body of pure water unattended with groves and other cheerful rural images by which fresh water is usually accompanied, and unable to give furtherance to the meagre vegetation around it—excites a sense of some repulsive power strongly put forth, and thus deepens the melancholy natural to such scenes. Nor is the feeling of solitude often more forcibly or more solemnly impressed than by the side of one of these mountain pools: though desolate and forbidding, it seems a distinct place to repair to; yet where the visitants must be rare, and there can be no disturbance. Water-fowl flock hither; and the lonely Angler may here be seen; but the imagination, not content with this scanty allowance of society, is tempted to attribute a voluntary power to every change which takes place in such a spot, whether it be the breeze that wanders over the surface of the water, or the splendid lights of evening resting upon it in the midst of awful precipices.

"There, sometimes does a leaping fish
Send through the tarn a lonely cheer;
The crags repeat the raven's croak
In symphony austere:
Thither the rainbow comes, the cloud,
And mists that spread the flying shroud,
And sunbeams, and the sounding blast."

It will be observed that this country is bounded on the south and east by the sea, which combines beautifully, from many elevated points, with the inland scenery; and, from the bay of Morcamb, the sloping shores and back-ground of distant mountains are seen, composing pictures equally distinguished for amenity and grandeur. But the estuaries on this coast are in a great measure bare at low water; and there is no instance of the sea running far up among the mountains, and mingling with the Lakes, which are such in the strict and usual sense of the word, being of fresh water. Nor have the streams, from the shortness of their course, time to acquire that body of water necessary to confer upon them much majesty. In fact, the most considerable, while they continue in the mountain and lake-country, are rather large brooks than rivers. The water is perfectly pellucid, through which in many places are seen, to a great depth, their beds of rock, or of blue gravel, which give to the water itself an exquisitely cerulean colour: this is particularly striking in the rivers Derwent and Duddon, which may be compared, such and so various are their beauties, to any two rivers of equal length of course in any country. The number of the torrents and smaller brooks is infinite, with their water-falls and water-breaks; and they need not here be described. I will only observe that, as many, even of the smallest rills, have either found, or made for themselves, recesses in the sides of the mountains or in the vales, they have tempted the primitive inhabitants to settle near them for shelter; and hence, cottages so placed, by seeming to withdraw from the eye, are the more endeared to the feelings.

The Woods consist chiefly of oak, ash, and birch, and here and there Wych-elm, with underwood of hazle, the white and black thorn, and hollies; in moist places alders and willows abound; and yews among the rocks. Formerly the whole country must have been covered with wood to a great height up the mountains; where native Scotch firs must have grown in great profusion, as they do in the northern part of Scotland to this day. But not one of these old inhabitants has existed, perhaps, for some hundreds of years; the beautiful traces, however, of the universal sylvan appearance the country formerly had, yet survive in the native coppice-woods that have been protected by inclosures, and also in the forest-trees and hollies, which, though disappearing fast, are yet scattered both over the inclosed and uninclosed parts of the mountains. The same is expressed by the beauty and intricacy with which the fields and coppice-woods are often intermingled: the plough of the first settlers having followed naturally the veins of richer, dryer, or less stony soil; and thus it has shaped out an intermixture of wood and lawn, with a grace and wildness which it would have been impossible for the hand of studied art to produce. Other trees have been introduced within these last fifty years, such as beeches, larches, limes and plantations of firs, seldom with advantage, and often with great injury to the appearance of the country; but the syca- more (which I believe was brought into this island from Germany, not more than two hundred years ago) has long been the favourite of the cottagers; and, with the fir, has been chosen to screen their dwellings: and is sometimes found in the fields whither the winds or the waters may have carried its seeds.

The want most felt, however, is that of timber trees. There are a few magnificent ones to be found near any of the lakes; and unless greater care be taken, there will, in a short time, scarcely be left an ancient oak that would repay the cost of felling. The neighbourhood of Rydal, notwithstanding the havoc which has been made, is yet nobly distinguished. In the woods of Lowther, also, is found an almost matchless store of ancient trees, and the majesty and wildness of the native forest.

Among the smaller vegetable ornaments must be reckoned the bilberry, a ground plant, never so beautiful as in early spring, when it is seen under bare or budding trees, that imperfectly intercept the sun-shine, covering the rocky knolls with a pure mantle of fresh verdure, more lively than the herbage of the open fields;—the broom that spreads luxuriantly along rough pastures, and in the month of June interveins the steep copses with its golden blossoms;—and the juniper, a rich evergreen, that thrives in spite of cattle, upon the uninclosed parts of the mountains:—the Dutch myrtle diffuses fragrance in moist places; and there is an endless variety of brilliant flowers in the fields and meadows, which, if the agriculture of the country were more carefully attended to, would disappear. Nor can I omit again to notice the lichens and mosses: their profusion, beauty, and variety exceed those of any other country I have seen.

It may now be proper to say a few words respecting climate, and "skiey influences," in which this region, as far as the character of its landscapes is affected by them, may, upon the whole, be considered fortunate. The country is, indeed, subject to much bad weather, and it has been ascertained that twice as much rain falls here as in many parts of the island; but the number of black drizzling days, that blot out the face of things, is by no means proportionally great. Nor is a continuance of thick, flagging, damp air so common as in the West of England and Ireland. The rain here comes down heartily, and is frequently succeeded by clear, bright weather, when every brook is vocal, and every torrent sonorous; brooks and torrents, which are never muddy, even in the heaviest floods, except, after a drought, they happen to be defiled for a short time by waters that have swept along dusty roads, or have broken out into ploughed fields. Days of unsettled weather, with partial showers, are very frequent; but the showers, darkening, or brightening, as they fly from hill to hill, are not less grateful to the eye than finely interwoven passages of gay and sad music are touching to the ear. Vapours exhaling from the lakes and meadows after sun-rise, in a hot season, or, in moist weather, brooding upon the heights, or descending towards the valleys with inaudible motion, give a visionary character to every thing around them; and are in themselves so beautiful, as to dispose us to enter into the feelings of those simple nations (such as the Laplanders of this day) by whom they are taken for guardian deities of the mountains; or to sympathize with others who have fancied these delicate apparitions to be the spirits of their departed ancestors. Akin to these are fleecy clouds resting upon the hill-tops; they are not easily managed in picture, with their accompaniments of blue sky; but how glorious are they in nature! how pregnant with imagination for the poet! and the height of the Cumbrian mountains is sufficient to exhibit daily and hourly instances of those mysterious attachments. Such clouds, cleaving to their stations, or lifting up suddenly their glittering heads from behind rocky barriers, or hurrying out of sight with speed of the sharpest edge—will often tempt an inhabitant to congratulate himself on belonging to a country of mists and clouds and storms, and make him think of the blank sky of Egypt, and of the cerulean vacancy of Italy, as an unanimated and even a sad spectacle. The atmosphere, however, as in every country subject to much rain, is frequently unfavourable to landscape, especially when keen winds succeed the rain which are apt to produce coldness, spottiness, and an unmeaning or repulsive detail in the distance;—a sunless frost, under a canopy of leaden and shapeless clouds, is, as far as it allows things to be seen, equally disagreeable.

It has been said that in human life there are moments worth ages. In a more subdued tone of sympathy may we affirm, that in the climate of England there are, for the lover of nature, days which are worth whole months,—I might say—even years. One of these favoured days some-times occurs in spring-time, when that soft air is breathing over the blossoms and new-born verdure, which inspired Buchanan with his beautiful Ode to the first of May; the air, which, in the luxuriance of his fancy, he likens to that of the golden age,—to that which gives motion to the funereal cypresses on the banks of Lethe;—to the air which is to salute beatified spirits when expiatory fires shall have consumed the earth with all her habitations. But it is in autumn that days of such affecting influence most frequently intervene;—the atmosphere seems refined, and the sky rendered more crystalline, as the vivifying heat of the year abates; the lights and shadows are more delicate; the colouring is richer and more finely harmonized; and, in this season of stillness, the ear being unoccupied, or only gently excited, the sense of vision becomes more susceptible of its appropriate enjoyments. A resident in a country like this which we are treating of, will agree with me, that the presence of a lake is indispens-able to exhibit in perfection the beauty of one of these days; and he must have experienced, while looking on the unruffled waters, that the imagination, by their aid, is carried into recesses of feeling otherwise impenetrable. The reason of this is, that the heavens are not only brought down into the bosom of the earth, but that the earth is mainly looked at, and thought of, through the medium of a purer element. The happiest times is when the equinoxial gales are departed; but their fury may probably be called to mind by the sight of a few shattered boughs, whose leaves do not differ in colour from the faded foliage of the stately oaks from which these relics of the storm depend: all else speaks of tranquillity;—not a breath of air, no restlessness of insects, and not a moving object perceptible—except the clouds gliding in the depths of the lake, or the traveller passing along, an inverted image, whose motion seems governed by the quiet of a time, to which its archetype, the living person, is, perhaps, insensible:—or it may happen, that the figure of one of the larger birds, a raven or a heron, is crossing silently among the reflected clouds, while the voice of the real bird, from the element aloft, gently awakens in the spectator the recollection of appetites and instincts, pursuits and occupations, that deform and agitate the world,—yet have no power to prevent Nature from putting on an aspect capable of satisfying the most intense cravings for the tranquil, the lovely, and the perfect, to which man, the noblest of her creatures, is subject.

Thus far, of climate, as influencing the feelings through its effect on the objects of sense. We may add, that whatever has been said upon the advantages derived to these scenes from a changeable atmosphere, would apply, perhaps still more forcibly, to their appearance under the varied solemnities of night. Milton, it will be remembered, has given a clouded moon to Paradise itself. In the night-season also, the narrowness of the vales, and comparative smallness of the lakes, are especially adapted to bring surrounding objects home to the eye and to the heart. The stars, taking their stations above the hill-tops, are contemplated from a spot like the Abyssinian recess of Rasselas, with much more touching interest than they are likely to excite when looked at from an open country with ordinary undulations: and it must be obvious, that it is the bays only of large lakes that can present such contrasts of light and shadow as those of smaller dimensions display from every quarter. A deep contracted valley, with diffused waters, such a valley and plains level and wide as those of Chaldea, are the two extremes in which the beauty of the heavens and their connexion with the earth are most sensibly felt. Nor do the advantages I have been speaking of imply here an exclusion of the aerial effects of distance. These are insured by the height of the mountains, and are found, even in the narrowest vales, where they lengthen in perspective, or act (if the expression may be used) as telescopes for the open country.

The subject would bear to be enlarged upon: but I will conclude this section with a nightscene suggested by the Vale of Keswick. The Fragment is well known; but it gratifies me to insert it, as the Writer was one of the first who led the way to a worthy admiration of this country.

> "Now sunk the sun, now twilight sunk, and night
> Rode in her zenith; not a passing breeze
> Sigh'd to the grove, which in the midnight air
> Stood motionless, and in the peaceful floods
> Inverted hung: for now the billows slept
> Along the shore, nor heav'd the deep; but spread
> A shining mirror to the moon's pale orb,
> Which, dim and waning, o'er the shadowy cliffs,

The solemn woods, and spiry mountain tops,
Her glimmering faintness threw: now every eye,
Oppress'd with toil, was drown'd in deep repose,
Save that the unseen Shepherd in his watch,
Propp'd on his crook, stood listening by the fold,
And gaz'd the starry vault, and pendant moon;
Nor voice, nor sound, broke on the deep serene;
But the soft murmur of soft-gushing rills,
Forth issuing from the mountain's distant steep,
(Unheard till now, and now scarce heard)
    proclaim'd
All things at rest, and imag'd the still voice
Of quiet, whispering in the ear of night."

Section Second: Aspect of the Country, as Affected by its Inhabitants

Hitherto I have chiefly spoken of the features by which nature has discriminated this country from others. I will now describe, in general terms, in what manner it is indebted to the hand of man. What I have to notice on this subject will emanate most easily and perspicuously from a description of the ancient and present inhabitants, their occupations, their condition of life, the distribution of landed property among them, and the tenure by which it is holden.

The reader will suffer me here to recall to his mind the shapes of the vallies, and their position with respect to each other, and the forms and substance of the intervening mountains. He will people the vallies with lakes and rivers: the coves and sides of the mountains with pools and torrents; and will bound half of the circle which we have contemplated by the sands of the sea, or by the sea itself. He will conceive that, from the point upon which he stood, he looks down upon this scene before the country had been penetrated by any inhabitants:—to vary his sensations, and to break in upon their stillness, he will form to himself an image of the tides visiting and re-visiting the friths, the main sea dashing against the bolder shore, the rivers pursuing their course to be lost in the mighty mass of waters. He may see or hear in fancy the winds sweeping over the lakes, or piping with a loud voice among the mountain peaks; and, lastly, may think of the primeval woods shedding and renewing their leaves with no human eye to notice, or human heart to regret or welcome the change. "When the first settlers entered this region (says an animated writer) they found it overspread with wood; forest trees, the fir, the oak, the ash, and the birch had skirted the fells, tufted the hills, and shaded the vallies, through centuries of silent solitude; the birds and beasts of prey reigned over the meeker species; and the bellum inter Omnia maintained the balance of nature in the empire of beasts."

Such was the state and appearance of this region when the aboriginal colonists of the Celtic tribes were first driven or drawn towards it, and became joint tenants with the wolf, the boar, the wild bull, the red deer, and the leigh, a gigantic species of deer which has been long extinct; while the inaccessible crags were occupied by the falcon, the raven, and the eagle. The inner parts were too secluded, and of too little value, to participate much of the benefit of Roman manners; and though these conquerors encouraged the Britons to the improvement of their lands in the plain country of Furness and Cumberland, they seem to have had little connexion with the mountains, except for military purposes, or in subservience to the profit they drew from the mines.

When the Romans retired from Great Britain, it is well known that these mountain-fastnesses furnished a protection to some unsubdued Britons, long after the more accessible and more fertile districts had been seized by the Saxon or Danish invader. A few, though distinct, traces of Roman forts or camps, as at Ambleside, and upon Dunmallet, and a few circles of rude stones attributed to the Druids, are theonly vestiges that remain upon the surface of the country, of these ancient occupants; and, as the Saxons and Danes, who succeeded to the possession of the villages and hamlets which had been established by the Britons, seem at first to have confined themselves to the open country,—we may descend at once to times long posterior to the conquest by the Normans, when their feudal polity was regularly established. We may easily conceive that these narrow dales and mountain sides, choked up as they must have been with wood, lying out of the way of communication with other parts of the Island, and upon the edge of a hostile kingdom, could have little attraction for the high-born and powerful; especially as the more open parts of the country furnished positions for castles and houses of defence, sufficient to repel any of those sudden attacks, which, in the then rude state of military knowledge, could be made upon them. Accordingly, the more retired regions (and to such I am now confining myself) must have been neglected or shunned even by the persons whose baronial or signioral rights extended over them, and left, doubtless, partly as a place of refuge for outlaws and robbers, and partly granted out for the more settled habitation of a few vassals following the employment of shepherds or woodlanders. Hence these lakes and inner vallies are unadorned by any remains of ancient grandeur, castles, or monastic edifices, which are only found upon the skirts of the country, as Furness Abbey, Calder Abbey, the Priory of Lannercost, Gleaston Castle,—long ago a residence of the Flemings,—and the numerous ancient castles of the Cliffords, the Lucys, and the Dacres. On the southern side of these mountains, (especially in that part known by the name of Furness Fells, which is more remote from the borders,) the state of society would necessarily be more settled; though it also was fashioned, not a little, by its neighbourhood to a hostile kingdom. We will, therefore, give a sketch of the economy of the Abbots in the distribution of lands among their tenants, as similar plans were doubtless adopted by other Lords, and as the consequences have affected the face of the country materially to the present day, being, in fact, one of the principal causes which give it such a striking superiority, in beauty and interest, over all other parts of the island.

"When the Abbots of Furness," says, an author before cited, "enfranchised their villains, and raised them to the dignity of customary tenants, the lands, which they had cultivated for their lord, were divided into whole tenements; each of which, besides the customary annual rent, was charged with the obligation of having in readiness a man completely armed for the king's service on the borders, or elsewhere; each of these whole tenements was again subdivided into four equal parts; each villain had one; and the party tenant contributed his share to the support of the man of arms, and of other burdens. These divisions were not properly distinguished; the land remained mixed; each tenant had a share through all the arable and meadow-land, and common of pasture over all the wastes. These sub-tenements were judged sufficient for the support of so many families; and no further division was permitted. These divisions and sub-divisions were convenient at the time for which they were calculated: the land, so parcelled out, was of necessity more attended to, and the industry greater, when more persons were to be supported by the produce of it. The frontier of the kingdom, within which Furness was considered, was in a constant state of attack and defence; more hands, therefore, were necessary to guard the coast, to repel an invasion from Scotland, or make reprisals on the hostile neighbour. The dividing the lands in such manner as has been shown, increased the number of inhabitants, and kept them at home till called for: and, the land being mixed, and the several tenants united in equipping the plough, the absence of the fourth man was no prejudice to the cultivation of his land, which was committed to the care of three.

While the villains of Low Furness were thus distributed over the land, and employed in agriculture; those of High Furness were charged with the care of flocks and herds, to protect them from the wolves which lurked in the thickets, and in winter to browze them with the tender sprouts of hollies and ash. This custom was not till lately discontinued in High Furness; and holly-trees were carefully preserved for that purpose when all other wood was cleared off; large tracts of common being so covered with these trees, as to have the appearance of a forest of hollies. At the Shepherd's call, the flocks surrounded the hollybush, and received the croppings at his hand, which they greedily nibbled up, bleating for more. The Abbots of Furness enfranchised these pastoral vassals, and permitted them to enclose quillets to their houses, for which they paid encroachment rent."—West's Antiquities of Furness.

However desirable, for the purposes of defence, a numerous population might be, it was not possible to make at once the same numerous allotments among the untilled vallies, and upon the sides of the mountains, as had been made in the cultivated plains. The enfranchised shepherd, or woodlander, having chosen there his place of residence, builds it of sods, or of the mountain-stone, and, with the permission of his lord, encloses, like Robinson Crusoe, a small croft or two immediately at his door for such animals as he wishes to protect. Others are happy to imitate his example, and avail themselves of the same privileges: and thus a population, mainly of Danish or Norse origin, as the dialect indicates, crept on towards the more secluded parts of the vallies. Chapels, daughters of some distant mother church, are first erected in the more open and fertile vales, as those of Bowness and Grasmere, offsets of Kendal: which again, after a period, as the settled population increases, become mother-churches to smaller edifices, planted, at length, in almost every dale throughout the country. The inclosures, formed by the tenantry, are for a long time confined to the home-steads; and the arable and meadow land of the vales is possessed in common field; the several portions being marked out by stones, bushes, or trees: which portions, where the custom has survived, to this day are called dales, from the word deylen, to distribute; but, while the valley was thus lying open, enclosures seem to have taken place upon the sides of the mountains; because the land there was not intermixed, and was of little comparative value; and, therefore, small opposition would be made to its being appropriated by those to whose habitations it was contiguous. Hence the singular appearance which the sides of many of these mountains exhibit, intersected, as they are, almost to the summit, with stone walls. When first erected, these stone fences must have little disfigured the face of the country; as part of the lines would every where be hidden by the quantity of native wood then remaining; and the lines would also be broken (as they still are) by the rocks which interrupt and vary their course. In the meadows, and in those parts of the lower grounds where the soil has not been sufficiently drained, and could not afford a stable foundation, there, when the increasing value of land,

and the inconvenience suffered from intermixed plots of ground in common field, had induced each inhabitant to enclose his own, they were compelled to make the fences of alders, willows, and other trees. These, where the native wood had disappeared, have frequently enriched the vallies with a sylvan appearance; while the intricate intermixture of property has given to the fences a graceful irregularity, which, where large properties are prevalent, and large capitals employed in agriculture, is unknown. This sylvan appearance is heightened by the number of ash-trees planted in rows along the quick fences, and along the walls, for the purpose of browzing the cattle at the approach of winter. The branches are lopped off and strewn upon the pastures; and when the cattle have stripped them of the leaves, they are used for repairing the hedges or for fuel.

We have thus seen a numerous body of Dalesmen creeping into possession of their home-steads, their little crofts, their mountain-enclosures; and, finally, the whole vale is visibly divided; except, perhaps, here and there some marshy ground, which, till fully drained, would not repay the trouble of enclosing. But these last partitions do not seem to have been general, till long after the pacification of the Borders, by the union of the two crowns: when the cause, which had first determined the distribution of land into such small parcels, had not only ceased,—but likewise a general improvement had taken place in the country, with a correspondent rise in the value of its produce. From the time of the union, it is certain that this species of feudal population must rapidly have diminished. That it was formerly much more numerous than it is at present, is evident from the multitude of tenements (I do not mean houses, but small divisions of land) which belonged formerly each to a several proprietor, and for which separate fines are paid to the manorial lord at this day. These are often in the proportion of four to one of the present occupants. "Sir Launcelot Threlkeld, who lived in the reign of Henry VII., was wont to say, he had three noble houses, one for pleasure, Crosby, in Westmoreland, where he had a park full of deer; one for profit and warmth, wherein to reside in winter, namely, Yanwith, nigh Penrith; and the third, Threlkeld, (on the edge of the vale of Keswick), well stocked with tenants to go with him to the wars." But, as I have said, from the union of the two crowns, this numerous vassalage (their services not being wanted) would rapidly diminish; various tenements would be united in one possessor; and the aboriginal houses, probably little better than hovels, like the kraels of savages, or the huts of the Highlanders of Scotland, would fall into decay, and the places of many be supplied by substantial and comfortable buildings, a majority of which remain to this day scattered over the vallies, and are often the only dwellings found in them.

From the time of the erection of these houses, till within the last sixty years, the state of society, though no doubt slowly and gradually improving, underwent no material change. Corn was grown in these vales (through which no carriage-road had yet been made) sufficient upon each estate to furnish bread for each family, and no more: notwithstanding the union of several tenements, the possessions of each inhabitant still being small, in the same field was seen an intermixture of different crops; and the plough was interrupted by little rocks, mostly overgrown with wood, or by spongy places, which the tillers of the soil had neither leisure nor capital to convert into firm land. The storms and moisture of the climate induced them to sprinkle their upland property with outhouses of native stone, as places of shelter for their sheep, where, in tempestuous weather, food was distributed to them. Every family spun from its own flock the wool with which it was clothed; a weaver was here and there found among them; and the rest of their wants was supplied by the produce of the yarn, which they carded and spun in their own houses, and carried to market, either under their arms, or more frequently on pack-horses, a small train taking their way weekly down the valley or over the mountains to the most commodious town. They had, as I have said, their rural chapel, and of course their minister, in clothing or in manner of life, in no respect differing from themselves, except on the Sabbath-day; this was the sole distinguished individual among them; every thing else, person and possession, exhibited a perfect equality, a community of shepherds and agriculturists, proprietors, for the most part, of the lands which they occupied and cultivated.

While the process above detailed was going on, the native forest must have been every where receding; but trees were planted for the sustenance of the flocks in winter,—such was then the rude state of agriculture; and, for the same cause, it was necessary that care should be taken of some part of the growth of the native woods. Accordingly, in Queen Elizabeth's time, this was so strongly felt, that a petition was made to the Crown, praying, "that the Blomaries in High Furness might be abolished, on account of the quantity of wood which was consumed in them for the use of the mines, to the great detriment of the cattle." But this same cause, about a hundred years after, produced effects directly contrary to those which had been deprecated. The re-establishment, at that period, of furnaces upon a large scale, made it the interest of the people to convert the steeper and more stony of the enclosures, sprinkled over with remains of the native forest, into close woods, which, when cattle and sheep were excluded, rapidly sowed and thickened themselves.

The reader's attention has been directed to the cause by which tufts of wood, pasturage, meadow, and arable land, with its various produce, are intricately intermingled in the same field; and he will now see, in like manner, how enclosures entirely of wood, and those of cultivated ground, are blended all over the country under a law of similar wildness.

An historic detail has thus been given of the manner in which the hand of man has acted upon the surface of the inner regions of this mountainous country, as incorporated with and subservient to the powers and processes of nature. We will now take a view of the same agency—acting, within narrower bounds, for the production of the few works of art and accommodations of life which, in so simple a state of society, could be necessary. These are merely habitations of man and coverts for beasts, roads and bridges, and places of worship.

And to begin with the COTTAGES. They are scattered over the vallies, and under the hill sides, and on the rocks; and, even to this day, in the more retired dales, without any intrusion of more assuming buildings;

> Cluster'd like stars some few, but single most,
> And lurking dimly in their shy retreats,
> Or glancing on each other cheerful looks,
> Like separated stars with clouds between.

The dwelling-houses, and contiguous outhouses, are, in many instances, of the colour of the native rock, out of which they have been built; but, frequently the Dwelling or Fire-house, as it is ordinarily called, has been distinguished from the barn or byer by rough-cast and white wash, which, as the inhabitants are not hasty in renewing it, in a few years acquires, by the influence of weather, a tint at once sober and variegated. As these houses have been, from father to son, inhabited by persons engaged in the same occupations, yet necessarily with changes in their circumstances, they have received without incongruity additions and accommodations adapted to the needs of each successive occupant, who, being for the most part proprietor, was at liberty to follow his own fancy: so that these humble dwellings remind the contemplative spectator of a production of nature, and may (using a strong expression) rather be said to have grown than to have been erected;—to have risen, by an instinct of their own, out of the native rock—so little is there in them of formality, such is their wildness and beauty. Among the numerous recesses and projections in the walls and in the different stages of their roofs, are seen bold and harmonious effects of contrasted sunshine and shadow. It is a favourable circumstance, that the strong winds, which sweep down the vallies, induced the inhabitants, at a time when the materials for building were easily procured, to furnish many of these dwellings with substantial porches; and such as have not this defence, are seldom unprovided with a projection of two large slates over their thresholds. Nor will the singular beauty of the chimneys escape the eye of the attentive traveller. Sometimes a low chimney, almost upon a level with the roof, is overlaid with a slate, supported upon four slender pillars, to prevent the wind from driving the smoke down the chimney. Others are of a quadrangular shape, rising one or two feet above the roof; which low square is often surmounted by a tall cylinder, giving to the cottage chimney the most beautiful shape in which it is ever seen. Nor will it be too fanciful or refined to remark, that there is a pleasing harmony between a tall chimney of this circular form, and the living column of smoke, ascending from it through the still air. These dwellings, mostly built, as has been said, of rough unhewn stone, are roofed with slates, which were rudely taken from the quarry before the present art of splitting them was understood, and are, therefore, rough and uneven in their surface, so that both the coverings and sides of the houses have furnished places of rest for the seeds of lichens, mosses, ferns, and flowers. Hence buildings, which in their very form call to mind the processes of nature, do thus, clothed in part with a vegetable garb, appear to be received into the bosom of the living principle of things, as it acts and exists among the woods and fields; and, by their colour and their shape, affectingly direct the thoughts to that tranquil course of nature and simplicity, along which the humble-minded inhabitants have, through so many generations, been led. Add the little garden with its shed for bee-hives, its small bed of pot-herbs, and its borders and patches of flowers for Sunday posies, with sometimes a choice few too much prized to be plucked; an orchard of proportioned size; a cheesepress, often supported by some tree near the door; a cluster of embowering sycamores for summer shade; with a tall fir, through which the winds sing when other trees are leafless; the little rill or household spout murmuring in all seasons;—combine these incidents and images together, and you have the representative idea of a mountain-cottage in this country so beautifully formed in itself, and so richly adorned by the hand of nature.

Till within the last sixty years there was no communication between any of these vales by carriage-roads; all bulky articles were transported on pack-horses. Owing, however, to the population not being concentrated in villages, but scattered, the vallies themselves were intersected as now by innumerable lanes and path-ways leading from house to house and from field to field. These lanes, where they are fenced by stone walls, are mostly bordered with ashes, hazels, wild roses, and beds of tall fern at their base; while the walls themselves, if old, are overspread with mosses, small ferns, wild strawberries, the geranium, and lichens: and, if the wall happen to rest against a bank of earth, it is sometimes almost wholly concealed by a rich facing of stone-fern. It is a great advantage to a traveller or resident, that these numerous lanes and paths, if he be a zealous admirer of nature, will lead him on into all the recesses of the country, so that the hidden treasures of its landscapes may, by an ever-ready guide, be laid open to his eyes.

Likewise to the smallness of the several properties is owing the great number of bridges over the brooks and torrents, and the daring and graceful neglect of danger or accommodation with which so many of them are constructed, the rudeness of the forms of some, and their endless variety. But, when I speak of this rudeness, I must at the same time add, that many of these structures are in themselves models of elegance, as if they had been formed upon principles of the most thoughtful architecture. It is to be regretted that these monuments of the skill of our ancestors, and of that happy instinct by which consummate beauty was produced, are disappearing fast; but sufficient specimens remain to give a high gratification to the man of genuine taste. Travellers who may not have been accustomed to pay attention to things so inobtrusive, will excuse me if I point out the proportion between the span and elevation of the arch, the lightness of the parapet, and the graceful manner in which its curve follows faithfully that of the arch.

Upon this subject I have nothing further to notice, except the PLACES OF WORSHIP, which have mostly a little school-house adjoining. The architecture of these churches and chapels, where they have not been recently rebuilt or modernised, is of a style not less appropriate and admirable than that of the dwelling houses and other structures. How sacred the spirit by which our forefathers were directed! The *religio loci* is no where violated by these unstinted, yet unpretending, works of human hands. They exhibit generally a well-proportioned oblong, with a suitable porch, in some instances a steeple tower, and in others nothing more than a small belfry, in which one or two bells hang visibly. But these objects, though pleasing in their forms, must necessarily, more than others in rural scenery, derive their interest from the sentiments of piety and reverence for the modest virtues and simple manners of humble life with which they may be contemplated. A man must be very insensible who would not be touched with pleasure at the sight of the chapel of Buttermere, so strikingly expressing, by its diminutive size, how small must be the congregation there assembled, as it were, like one family; and proclaiming at the same time to the passenger, in connection with the surrounding mountains, the depth of that seclusion in which the people live, that has rendered necessary the building of a separate place of worship for so few. A patriot, calling to mind the images of the stately fabrics of Canterbury, York, or Westminster, will find a heart-felt satisfaction in presence of this lowly pile, as a monument of the wise institutions of our country, and as evidence of the all-pervading and paternal care of that venerable Establishment, of which it is, perhaps, the humblest daughter. The edifice is scarcely larger than many of the single stones or fragments of rock which are scattered near it.

We have thus far confined our observations on this division of the subject, to that part of these Dales which runs up far into the mountains.

As we descend towards the open country, we meet with halls and mansions, many of which have been places of defence against the incursions of the Scottish borderers; and they not unfrequently retain their towers and battlements. To these houses, parks are sometimes attached, and to their successive proprietors we chiefly owe whatever ornament is still left to the country of majestic timber. Through the open parts of the vales are scattered, also, houses of a middle rank between the pastoral cottage and the old hall residence of the knight or esquire. Such houses differ much from the rugged cottages before described, and are generally graced with a little court or garden in front, where may yet be seen specimens of those fantastic and quaint figures which our ancestors were fond of shaping out in yew-tree, holly, or box-wood. The passenger will sometimes smile at such elaborate display of petty art, while the house does not deign to look upon the natural beauty or the sublimity which its situation almost unavoidably commands.

Thus has been given a faithful description, the minuteness of which the reader will pardon, of the face of this country as it was, and had been through centuries, till within the last sixty years. Towards the head of these Dales was found a perfect Republic of Shepherds and Agriculturists, among whom the plough of each man was confined to the maintenance of his own family, or to the occasional accommodation of his neighbour. Two or three cows furnished each family with milk and cheese. The chapel was the only edifice that presided over these dwellings, the supreme head of this pure Commonwealth; the members of which existed in the midst of a powerful empire like an ideal society or an organized community, whose constitution had been imposed and regulated by the mountains which protected it. Neither high-born nobleman, knight, nor esquire was here; but many of these humble sons of the hills had a consciousness that the land, which they walked over and tilled, had for more than five hundred years been possessed by men of their name and blood; and venerable was the transition, when a curious traveller, descending from the heart of the mountains, had come to some ancient manorial residence in the more open parts of the Vales, which, through the rights attached to its proprietor, connected the almost visionary mountain republic he had been contemplating with the substantial frame of society as existing in the laws and constitution of a mighty empire.

⁂

Anecdote for Fathers, Showing How the Practice of Lying May Be Taught

I have a boy of five years old;
His face is fair and fresh to see;
His limbs are cast in beauty's mould,
And dearly he loves me.

One morn we strolled on our dry walk,
Our quiet home all full in view,
And held such intermitted talk
As we are wont to do.

My thoughts on former pleasures ran;
I thought of Kilve's delightful shore,
Our pleasant home when spring began,
A long, long year before.

A day it was when I could bear
Some fond regrets to entertain;
With so much happiness to spare,
I could not feel a pain.

The green earth echoed to the feet
Of lambs that bounded through the glade,

From shade to sunshine, and as fleet
From sunshine back to shade.

Birds warbled round me—and each trace
Of inward sadness had its charm;
Kilve, thought I, was a favoured place,
And so is Liswyn farm.

My boy beside me tripped, so slim
And graceful in his rustic dress!
And, as we talked, I questioned him,
In very idleness.

"Now tell me, had you rather be,"
I said, and took him by the arm,
"On Kilve's smooth shore, by the green sea,
Or here at Liswyn farm?"

In careless mood he looked at me,
While still I held him by the arm,
And said, "At Kilve I'd rather be
Than here at Liswyn farm."

"Now, little Edward, say why so:
My little Edward, tell me why."—
"I cannot tell, I do not know."—
"Why, this is strange," said I;

"For, here are woods, hills smooth and warm:
There surely must some reason be
Why you would change sweet Liswyn farm
For Kilve by the green sea."

At this, my boy hung down his head,
He blushed with shame, nor made reply;
And three times to the child I said,
"Why, Edward, tell me why?"

His head he raised—there was in sight,
It caught his eye, he saw it plain—
Upon the house-top, glittering bright,
A broad and gilded vane.

Then did the boy his tongue unlock,
And eased his mind with this reply:
"At Kilve there was no weather-cock;
And that's the reason why."

O dearest, dearest boy! my heart
For better lore would seldom yearn,
Could I but teach the hundredth part
Of what from thee I learn.

Lines Written in Early Spring

I heard a thousand blended notes,
While in a grove I sate reclined,
In that sweet mood when pleasant thoughts
Bring sad thoughts to the mind.

To her fair works did Nature link
The human soul that through me ran;
And much it grieved my heart to think
What man has made of man.

Through primrose tufts, in that green bower,
The periwinkle trailed its wreaths;
And 'tis my faith that every flower
Enjoys the air it breathes.

The birds around me hopped and played,
Their thoughts I cannot measure:—
But the least motion which they made,
It seemed a thrill of pleasure.

The budding twigs spread out their fan,
To catch the breezy air;
And I must think, do all I can,
That there was pleasure there.

If this belief from heaven be sent,
If such be Nature's holy plan,
Have I not reason to lament
What man has made of man?

To My Sister

It is the first mild day of March:
Each minute sweeter than before
The redbreast sings from the tall larch
That stands beside our door.

There is a blessing in the air,
Which seems a sense of joy to yield
To the bare trees, and mountains bare,
And grass in the green field.

My sister! ('tis a wish of mine)
Now that our morning meal is done,
Make haste, your morning task resign;
Come forth and feel the sun.

Edward will come with you;—and, pray,
Put on with speed your woodland dress;
And bring no book: for this one day
We'll give to idleness.

No joyless forms shall regulate
Our living calendar:
We from to-day, my Friend, will date
The opening of the year.

Love, now a universal birth,
From heart to heart is stealing,
From earth to man, from man to earth:
—It is the hour of feeling.

One moment now may give us more
Than years of toiling reason:
Our minds shall drink at every pore
The spirit of the season.

Some silent laws our hearts will make,
Which they shall long obey:
We for the year to come may take
Our temper from to-day.

And from the blessed power that rolls
About, below, above,
We'll frame the measure of our souls:
They shall be tuned to love.

Then come, my Sister! come, I pray,
With speed put on your woodland dress;
And bring no book: for this one day
We'll give to idleness.

Expostulation and Reply

"Why, William, on that old grey stone,
Thus for the length of half a day,
Why, William, sit you thus alone,
And dream your time away?

"Where are your books?—that light bequeathed
To Beings else forlorn and blind!
Up! up! and drink the spirit breathed
From dead men to their kind.

"You look round on your Mother Earth,
As if she for no purpose bore you;
As if you were her first-born birth,
And none had lived before you!"

One morning thus, by Esthwaite lake,
When life was sweet, I knew not why,
To me my good friend Matthew spake,
And thus I made reply.

"The eye—it cannot choose but see;
We cannot bid the ear be still;
Our bodies feel, where'er they be,
Against or with our will.

"Nor less I deem that there are Powers
Which of themselves our minds impress;
That we can feed this mind of ours
In a wise passiveness.

"Think you,'mid all this mighty sum
Of things for ever speaking,
That nothing of itself will come,
But we must still be seeking?

"—Then ask not wherefore, here, alone,
Conversing as I may,
I sit upon this old grey stone,
And dream my time away."

The Tables Turned: An Evening Scene on the Same Subject

Up! up! my Friend, and quit your books;
Or surely you'll grow double:
Up! up! my Friend, and clear your looks;
Why all this toil and trouble?

The sun, above the mountain's head,
A freshening lustre mellow
Through all the long green fields has spread,
His first sweet evening yellow.

Books! 'tis a dull and endless strife:
Come, hear the woodland linnet,
How sweet his music! on my life,
There's more of wisdom in it.

And hark! how blithe the throstle sings!
He, too, is no mean preacher:
Come forth into the light of things,
Let Nature be your Teacher.

She has a world of ready wealth,
Our minds and hearts to bless—
Spontaneous wisdom breathed by health,
Truth breathed by cheerfulness.

One impulse from a vernal wood
May teach you more of man,
Of moral evil and of good,
Than all the sages can.

Sweet is the lore which Nature brings;
Our meddling intellect
Mis-shapes the beauteous forms of things:—
We murder to dissect.

Enough of Science and of Art;
Close up those barren leaves;
Come forth, and bring with you a heart
That watches and receives.

Lines Composed a Few Miles above Tintern Abbey

Five years have past; five summers, with the length
Of five long winters! and again I hear
These waters, rolling from their mountain-springs
With a soft inland murmur.—Once again
Do I behold these steep and lofty cliffs,
That on a wild secluded scene impress
Thoughts of more deep seclusion; and connect
The landscape with the quiet of the sky.
The day is come when I again repose
Here, under this dark sycamore, and view
These plots of cottage-ground, these orchard-tufts,
Which at this season, with their unripe fruits,
Are clad in one green hue, and lose themselves
'Mid groves and copses. Once again I see
These hedge-rows, hardly hedge-rows, little lines
Of sportive wood run wild: these pastoral farms,
Green to the very door; and wreaths of smoke
Sent up, in silence, from among the trees!
With some uncertain notice, as might seem
Of vagrant dwellers in the houseless woods,
Or of some Hermit's cave, where by his fire
The Hermit sits alone.

                              These beauteous forms,
Through a long absence, have not been to me
As is a landscape to a blind man's eye:
But oft, in lonely rooms, and 'mid the din
Of towns and cities, I have owed to them,
In hours of weariness, sensations sweet,
Felt in the blood, and felt along the heart;
And passing even into my purer mind,
With tranquil restoration:—feelings too
Of unremembered pleasure: such, perhaps,

As have no slight or trivial influence
On that best portion of a good man's life,
His little, nameless, unremembered, acts
Of kindness and of love. Nor less, I trust,
To them I may have owed another gift,
Of aspect more sublime; that blessed mood,
In which the burthen of the mystery,
In which the heavy and the weary weight
Of all this unintelligible world,
Is lightened:—that serene and blessed mood,
In which the affections gently lead us on,—
Until, the breath of this corporeal frame
And even the motion of our human blood
Almost suspended, we are laid asleep
In body, and become a living soul:
While with an eye made quiet by the power
Of harmony, and the deep power of joy,
We see into the life of things.

                                        If this
Be but a vain belief, yet, oh! how oft—
In darkness and amid the many shapes
Of joyless daylight; when the fretful stir
Unprofitable, and the fever of the world,
Have hung upon the beatings of my heart—
How oft, in spirit, have I turned to thee,
O sylvan Wye! thou wanderer thro' the woods,
How often has my spirit turned to thee!

And now, with gleams of half-extinguished thought,
With many recognitions dim and faint,
And somewhat of a sad perplexity,
The picture of the mind revives again:
While here I stand, not only with the sense
Of present pleasure, but with pleasing thoughts

That in this moment there is life and food
For future years. And so I dare to hope,
Though changed, no doubt, from what I was when
    first
I came among these hills; when like a roe
I bounded o'er the mountains, by the sides
Of the deep rivers, and the lonely streams,
Wherever nature led: more like a man
Flying from something that he dreads, than one
Who sought the thing he loved. For nature then
(The coarser pleasures of my boyish days,
And their glad animal movements all gone by)
To me was all in all.—I cannot paint
What then I was. The sounding cataract
Haunted me like a passion: the tall rock,
The mountain, and the deep and gloomy wood,
Their colours and their forms, were then to me
An appetite; a feeling and a love,
That had no need of a remoter charm,
By thought supplied, nor any interest
Unborrowed from the eye.—That time is past,
And all its aching joys are now no more,
And all its dizzy raptures. Not for this
Faint I, nor mourn nor murmur; other gifts
Have followed; for such loss, I would believe,
Abundant recompence. For I have learned
To look on nature, not as in the hour
Of thoughtless youth; but hearing oftentimes
The still, sad music of humanity,
Nor harsh nor grating, though of ample power
To chasten and subdue. And I have felt
A presence that disturbs me with the joy
Of elevated thoughts; a sense sublime
Of something far more deeply interfused,

Whose dwelling is the light of setting suns,
And the round ocean and the living air,
And the blue sky, and in the mind of man:
A motion and a spirit, that impels
All thinking things, all objects of all thought,
And rolls through all things. Therefore am I still
A lover of the meadows and the woods,
And mountains; and of all that we behold
From this green earth; of all the mighty world
Of eye, and ear,—both what they half create,
And what perceive; well pleased to recognise
In nature and the language of the sense,
The anchor of my purest thoughts, the nurse,
The guide, the guardian of my heart, and soul
Of all my moral being.

                        Nor perchance,
If I were not thus taught, should I the more
Suffer my genial spirits to decay:
For thou art with me here upon the banks
Of this fair river; thou my dearest Friend,
My dear, dear Friend; and in thy voice I catch
The language of my former heart, and read
My former pleasures in the shooting lights
Of thy wild eyes, Oh! yet a little while
May I behold in thee what I was once,
My dear, dear Sister! and this prayer I make,
Knowing that Nature never did betray
The heart that loved her; 'tis her privilege,
Through all the years of this our life, to lead
From joy to joy: for she can so inform
The mind that is within us, so impress
With quietness and beauty, and so feed
With lofty thoughts, that neither evil tongues,

Rash judgments, nor the sneers of selfish men,
Nor greetings where no kindness is, nor all
The dreary intercourse of daily life,
Shall e'er prevail against us, or disturb
Our cheerful faith, that all which we behold
Is full of blessings. Therefore let the moon
Shine on thee in thy solitary walk;
And let the misty mountain-winds be free
To blow against thee: and, in after years,
When these wild ecstasies shall be matured
Into a sober pleasure; when thy mind
Shall be a mansion for all lovely forms,
Thy memory be as a dwelling-place
For all sweet sounds and harmonies; oh! then,
If solitude, or fear, or pain, or grief,
Should be thy portion, with what healing thoughts
Of tender joy wilt thou remember me,
And these my exhortations! Nor, perchance—
If I should be where I no more can hear
Thy voice, nor catch from thy wild eyes these gleams
Of past existence—wilt thou then forget
That on the banks of this delightful stream
We stood together; and that I, so long
A worshipper of Nature, hither came
Unwearied in that service: rather say
With warmer love—oh! with far deeper zeal
Of holier love. Nor wilt thou then forget,
That after many wanderings, many years
Of absence, these steep woods and lofty cliffs,
And this green pastoral landscape, were to me
More dear, both for themselves and for thy sake!

The Old Cumberland Beggar

I saw an aged Beggar in my walk;
And he was seated, by the highway side,
On a low structure of rude masonry
Built at the foot of a huge hill, that they
Who lead their horses down the steep rough road
May thence remount at ease. The aged Man
Had placed his staff across the broad smooth stone
That overlays the pile; and, from a bag
All white with flour, the dole of village dames,
He drew his scraps and fragments, one by one;
And scanned them with a fixed and serious look
Of idle computation. In the sun,
Upon the second step of that small pile,
Surrounded by those wild unpeopled hills,
He sat, and ate his food in solitude:
And ever, scattered from his palsied hand,
That, still attempting to prevent the waste,
Was baffled still, the crumbs in little showers
Fell on the ground; and the small mountain birds,
Not venturing yet to peck their destined meal,
Approached within the length of half his staff.

Him from my childhood have I known; and then
He was so old, he seems not older now;
He travels on, a solitary Man,
So helpless in appearance, that for him
The sauntering Horseman throws not with a slack
And careless hand his alms upon the ground,
But stops,—that he may safely lodge the coin
Within the old Man's hat; nor quits him so,
But still, when he has given his horse the rein,
Watches the aged Beggar with a look
Sidelong, and half-reverted. She who tends

The toll-gate, when in summer at her door
She turns her wheel, if on the road she sees
The aged beggar coming, quits her work,
And lifts the latch for him that he may pass.
The post-boy, when his rattling wheels o'ertake
The aged Beggar in the woody lane,
Shouts to him from behind; and, if thus warned
The old man does not change his course, the boy
Turns with less noisy wheels to the roadside,
And passes gently by, without a curse
Upon his lips, or anger at his heart.

He travels on, a solitary Man;
His age has no companion. On the ground
His eyes are turned, and, as he moves along,
'They' move along the ground; and, evermore,
Instead of common and habitual sight
Of fields with rural works, of hill and dale,
And the blue sky, one little span of earth
Is all his prospect. Thus, from day to day,
Bow-bent, his eyes for ever on the ground,
He plies his weary journey; seeing still,
And seldom knowing that he sees, some straw,
Some scattered leaf, or marks which, in one
    track,
The nails of cart or chariot-wheel have left
Impressed on the white road,—in the same line,
At distance still the same. Poor Traveller!
His staff trails with him; scarcely do his feet
Disturb the summer dust; he is so still
In look and motion, that the cottage curs,
Ere he has passed the door, will turn away,
Weary of barking at him. Boys and girls,
The vacant and the busy, maids and youths,

And urchins newly breeched—all pass him by:
Him even the slow-paced waggon leaves behind.

But deem not this Man useless.—Statesmen! ye
Who are so restless in your wisdom, ye
Who have a broom still ready in your hands
To rid the world of nuisances; ye proud,
Heart-swoln, while in your pride ye contemplate
Your talents, power, or wisdom, deem him not
A burthen of the earth! 'Tis nature's law
That none, the meanest of created things,
Of forms created the most vile and brute,
The dullest or most noxious, should exist
Divorced from good—a spirit and pulse of good,
A life and soul, to every mode of being
Inseparably linked. Then be assured
That least of all can aught—that ever owned
The heaven-regarding eye and front sublime
Which man is born to—sink, howe'er depressed,
So low as to be scorned without a sin;
Without offence to God cast out of view;
Like the dry remnant of a garden-flower
Whose seeds are shed, or as an implement
Worn out and worthless. While from door to door
This old Man creeps, the villagers in him
Behold a record which together binds
Past deeds and offices of charity,
Else unremembered, and so keeps alive
The kindly mood in hearts which lapse of years,
And that half-wisdom half-experience gives,
Make slow to feel, and by sure steps resign
To selfishness and cold oblivious cares.
Among the farms and solitary huts,
Hamlets and thinly-scattered villages,

Where'er the aged Beggar takes his rounds,
The mild necessity of use compels
To acts of love; and habit does the work
Of reason; yet prepares that after-joy
Which reason cherishes. And thus the soul,
By that sweet taste of pleasure unpursued
Doth find herself insensibly disposed
To virtue and true goodness.

                              Some there are,
By their good works exalted, lofty minds
And meditative, authors of delight
And happiness, which to the end of time
Will live, and spread, and kindle: even such minds
In childhood, from this solitary Being,
Or from like wanderer, haply have received
(A thing more precious far than all that books
Or the solicitudes of love can do!)
That first mild touch of sympathy and thought,
In which they found their kindred with a world
Where want and sorrow were. The easy man
Who sits at his own door,—and, like the pear
That overhangs his head from the green wall,
Feeds in the sunshine; the robust and young,
The prosperous and unthinking, they who live
Sheltered, and flourish in a little grove
Of their own kindred;—all behold in him
A silent monitor, which on their minds
Must needs impress a transitory thought
Of self-congratulation, to the heart
Of each recalling his peculiar boons,
His charters and exemptions; and, perchance,
Though he to no one give the fortitude
And circumspection needful to preserve

His present blessings, and to husband up
The respite of the season, he, at least,
And 'tis no vulgar service, makes them felt.

Yet further.—Many, I believe, there are
Who live a life of virtuous decency,
Men who can hear the Decalogue and feel
No self-reproach; who of the moral law
Established in the land where they abide
Are strict observers; and not negligent
In acts of love to those with whom they dwell,
Their kindred, and the children of their blood.
Praise be to such, and to their slumbers peace!
—But of the poor man ask, the abject poor;
Go, and demand of him, if there be here
In this cold abstinence from evil deeds,
And these inevitable charities,
Wherewith to satisfy the human soul?
No—man is dear to man; the poorest poor
Long for some moments in a weary life
When they can know and feel that they have been,
Themselves, the fathers and the dealers-out
Of some small blessings; have been kind to such
As needed kindness, for this single cause,
That we have all of us one human heart.
—Such pleasure is to one kind Being known,
My neighbour, when with punctual care,
   each week
Duly as Friday comes, though pressed herself
By her own wants, she from her store of meal
Takes one unsparing handful for the scrip
Of this old Mendicant, and, from her door
Returning with exhilarated heart,
Sits by her fire, and builds her hope in heaven.

Then let him pass, a blessing on his head!
And while in that vast solitude to which
The tide of things has borne him, he appears
To breathe and live but for himself alone,
Unblamed, uninjured, let him bear about
The good which the benignant law of Heaven
Has hung around him: and, while life is his,
Still let him prompt the unlettered villagers
To tender offices and pensive thoughts.
—Then let him pass, a blessing on his head!
And, long as he can wander, let him breathe
The freshness of the valleys; let his blood
Struggle with frosty air and winter snows;
And let the chartered wind that sweeps the heath
Beat his grey locks against his withered face.
Reverence the hope whose vital anxiousness
Gives the last human interest to his heart.
May never HOUSE, misnamed of INDUSTRY,
Make him a captive!—for that pent-up din,
Those life-consuming sounds that clog the air,
Be his the natural silence of old age!
Let him be free of mountain solitudes;
And have around him, whether heard or not,
The pleasant melody of woodland birds.
Few are his pleasures: if his eyes have now
Been doomed so long to settle upon earth
That not without some effort they behold
The countenance of the horizontal sun,
Rising or setting, let the light at least
Find a free entrance to their languid orbs.
And let him, 'where' and 'when' he will, sit down
Beneath the trees, or on a grassy bank
Of highway side, and with the little birds
Share his chance-gathered meal; and, finally,

As in the eye of Nature he has lived,
So in the eye of Nature let him die!

Animal Tranquillity and Decay

The little hedgerow birds,
That peck along the road, regard him not.
He travels on, and in his face, his step,
His gait, is one expression: every limb,
His look and bending figure, all bespeak
A man who does not move with pain, but moves
With thought.—He is insensibly subdued
To settled quiet: he is one by whom
All effort seems forgotten; one to whom
Long patience hath such mild composure given,
That patience now doth seem a thing of which
He hath no need. He is by nature led
To peace so perfect that the young behold
With envy, what the Old Man hardly feels.

The Simplon Pass

                              —Brook and road
Were fellow-travellers in this gloomy Pass,
And with them did we journey several hours
At a slow step. The immeasurable height
Of woods decaying, never to be decayed,
The stationary blasts of waterfalls,
And in the narrow rent, at every turn,
Winds thwarting winds bewildered and forlorn,
The torrents shooting from the clear blue sky,
The rocks that muttered close upon our ears,
Black drizzling crags that spake by the wayside
As if a voice were in them, the sick sight
And giddy prospect of the raving stream,

The unfettered clouds and region of the heavens,
Tumult and peace, the darkness and the light—
Were all like workings of one mind, the features
Of the same face, blossoms upon one tree,
Characters of the great Apocalypse,
The types and symbols of Eternity,
Of first, and last, and midst, and without end.

Nutting

                              —It seems a day
(I speak of one from many singled out)
One of those heavenly days that cannot die;
When, in the eagerness of boyish hope,
I left our cottage-threshold, sallying forth
With a huge wallet o'er my shoulders slung,
A nutting-crook in hand; and turned my steps
Tow'rd some far-distant wood, a Figure quaint,
Tricked out in proud disguise of cast-off weeds
Which for that service had been husbanded,
By exhortation of my frugal Dame—
Motley accoutrement, of power to smile
At thorns, and brakes, and brambles,—and, in truth,
More ragged than need was! O'er pathless rocks,
Through beds of matted fern, and tangled thickets,
Forcing my way, I came to one dear nook
Unvisited, where not a broken bough
Drooped with its withered leaves, ungracious sign
Of devastation; but the hazels rose
Tall and erect, with tempting clusters hung,
A virgin scene!—A little while I stood,
Breathing with such suppression of the heart
As joy delights in; and, with wise restraint
Voluptuous, fearless of a rival, eyed

The banquet;—or beneath the trees I sate
Among the flowers, and with the flowers I played;
A temper known to those, who, after long
And weary expectation, have been blest
With sudden happiness beyond all hope.
Perhaps it was a bower beneath whose leaves
The violets of five seasons re-appear
And fade, unseen by any human eye;
Where fairy water-breaks do murmur on
For ever; and I saw the sparkling foam,
And—with my cheek on one of those green stones
That, fleeced with moss, under the shady trees,
Lay round me, scattered like a flock of sheep—
I heard the murmur and the murmuring sound,
In that sweet mood when pleasure loves to pay
Tribute to ease; and, of its joy secure,
The heart luxuriates with indifferent things,
Wasting its kindliness on stocks and stones,
And on the vacant air. Then up I rose,
And dragged to earth both branch and bough, with
    crash
And merciless ravage: and the shady nook
Of hazels, and the green and mossy bower,
Deformed and sullied, patiently gave up
Their quiet being: and, unless I now
Confound my present feelings with the past;
Ere from the mutilated bower I turned
Exulting, rich beyond the wealth of kings,
I felt a sense of pain when I beheld
The silent trees, and saw the intruding sky.—
Then, dearest Maiden, move along these shades
In gentleness of heart; with gentle hand
Touch—for there is a spirit in the woods.

She Dwelt Among the Untrodden Ways

She Dwelt among the untrodden ways
    Beside the springs of Dove,
A Maid whom there were none to praise
    And very few to love:

A violet by a mossy stone
    Half hidden from the eye!
—Fair as a star, when only one
    Is shining in the sky.

She lived unknown, and few could know
    When Lucy ceased to be;
But she is in her grave, and, oh,
    The difference to me!

I Travelled Among Unknown Men

I travelled among unknown men,
    In lands beyond the sea;
Nor, England! did I know till then
    What love I bore to thee.

'Tis past, that melancholy dream!
    Nor will I quit thy shore
A second time; for still I seem
    To love thee more and more.

Among thy mountains did I feel
    The joy of my desire;
And she I cherished turned her wheel
    Beside an English fire.

Thy mornings showed, thy nights concealed
    The bowers where Lucy played;
And thine too is the last green field
    That Lucy's eyes surveyed.

A Poet's Epitaph

Art thou a Statist in the van
Of public conflicts trained and bred?
—First learn to love one living man;
Then may'st thou think upon the dead.

A Lawyer art thou?—draw not nigh!
Go, carry to some fitter place
The keenness of that practised eye,
The hardness of that sallow face.

Art thou a Man of purple cheer?
A rosy Man, right plump to see?
Approach; yet, Doctor, not too near,
This grave no cushion is for thee.

Or art thou one of gallant pride,
A Soldier and no man of chaff?
Welcome!—but lay thy sword aside,
And lean upon a peasant's staff.

Physician art thou?—one, all eyes,
Philosopher!—a fingering slave,
One that would peep and botanize
Upon his mother's grave?

Wrapt closely in thy sensual fleece,
O turn aside,—and take, I pray,
That he below may rest in peace,
Thy ever-dwindling soul, away!

A Moralist perchance appears;
Led, Heaven knows how! to this poor sod:
And he has neither eyes nor ears;
Himself his world, and his own God;

One to whose smooth-rubbed soul can cling
Nor form, nor feeling, great or small;

A reasoning, self-sufficing thing,
An intellectual All-in-all!

Shut close the door; press down the latch;
Sleep in thy intellectual crust;
Nor lose ten tickings of thy watch
Near this unprofitable dust.

But who is He, with modest looks,
And clad in homely russet brown?
He murmurs near the running brooks
A music sweeter than their own.
He is retired as noontide dew,
Or fountain in a noon-day grove;
And you must love him, ere to you
He will seem worthy of your love.

The outward shows of sky and earth,
Of hill and valley, he has viewed;
And impulses of deeper birth
Have come to him in solitude.

In common things that round us lie
Some random truths he can impart,—
The harvest of a quiet eye
That broods and sleeps on his own heart.

But he is weak; both Man and Boy,
Hath been an idler in the land;
Contented if he might enjoy
The things which others understand.

—Come hither in thy hour of strength;
Come, weak as is a breaking wave!
Here stretch thy body at full length;
Or build thy house upon this grave.

The Fountain

We talked with open heart, and tongue
Affectionate and true,
A pair of friends, though I was young,
And Matthew seventy-two.

We lay beneath a spreading oak,
Beside a mossy seat;
And from the turf a fountain broke,
And gurgled at our feet.

"Now, Matthew!" said I, "let us match
This water's pleasant tune
With some old border-song, or catch
That suits a summer's noon;

"Or of the church-clock and the chimes
Sing here beneath the shade,
That half-mad thing of witty rhymes
Which you last April made!"

In silence Matthew lay, and eyed
The spring beneath the tree;
And thus the dear old Man replied,
The grey-haired man of glee:

"No check, no stay, this Streamlet fears;
How merrily it goes!
'Twill murmur on a thousand years,
And flow as now it flows.

"And here, on this delightful day,
I cannot choose but think
How oft, a vigorous man, I lay
Beside this fountain's brink.

"My eyes are dim with childish tears,
My heart is idly stirred,

For the same sound is in my ears
Which in those days I heard.

"Thus fares it still in our decay:
And yet the wiser mind
Mourns less for what age takes away
Than what it leaves behind.

"The blackbird amid leafy trees,
The lark above the hill,
Let loose their carols when they please,
Are quiet when they will.

"With Nature never do they wage
A foolish strife; they see
A happy youth, and their old age
Is beautiful and free:

"But we are pressed by heavy laws;
And often, glad no more,
We wear a face of joy, because
We have been glad of yore.

"If there be one who need bemoan
His kindred laid in earth,
The household hearts that were his own;
It is the man of mirth.

"My days, my Friend, are almost gone,
My life has been approved,
And many love me; but by none
Am I enough beloved."

"Now both himself and me he wrongs,
The man who thus complains!
I live and sing my idle songs
Upon these happy plains;

"And, Matthew, for thy children dead
I'll be a son to thee!"
At this he grasped my hand, and said,
"Alas! that cannot be."

We rose up from the fountain-side;
And down the smooth descent
Of the green sheep-track did we glide;
And through the wood we went;

And, ere we came to Leonard's rock,
He sang those witty rhymes
About the crazy old church-clock,
And the bewildered chimes.

Lucy Gray

Oft I had heard of Lucy Gray:
And, when I crossed the wild,
I chanced to see at break of day
The solitary child.

No mate, no comrade Lucy knew;
She dwelt on a wide moor,
—The sweetest thing that ever grew
Beside a human door!

You yet may spy the fawn at play,
The hare upon the green;
But the sweet face of Lucy Gray
Will never more be seen.

"To-night will be a stormy night—
You to the town must go;
And take a lantern, Child, to light
Your mother through the snow."

"That, Father! will I gladly do:
'Tis scarcely afternoon—
The minster-clock has just struck two,
And yonder is the moon!"

At this the Father raised his hook,
And snapped a faggot-band;
He plied his work;—and Lucy took
The lantern in her hand.

Not blither is the mountain roe:
With many a wanton stroke
Her feet disperse the powdery snow,
That rises up like smoke.

The storm came on before its time:
She wandered up and down;
And many a hill did Lucy climb
But never reached the town.

The wretched parents all that night
Went shouting far and wide;
But there was neither sound nor sight
To serve them for a guide.

At day-break on a hill they stood
That overlooked the moor;
And thence they saw the bridge of wood,
A furlong from their door.

They wept—and, turning homeward,
    cried,
"In heaven we all shall meet;"
—When in the snow the mother spied
The print of Lucy's feet.

Then downwards from the steep hill's edge
They tracked the footmarks small;

And through the broken hawthorn hedge,
And by the long stone-wall;

And then an open field they crossed:
The marks were still the same;
They tracked them on, nor ever lost;
And to the bridge they came.

They followed from the snowy bank
Those footmarks, one by one,
Into the middle of the plank;
And further there were none!

—Yet some maintain that to this day
She is a living child;
That you may see sweet Lucy Gray
Upon the lonesome wild.

O'er rough and smooth she trips along,
And never looks behind;
And sings a solitary song
That whistles in the wind.

Michael: A Pastoral Poem

If from the public way you turn your steps
Up the tumultuous brook of Green-head Ghyll,
You will suppose that with an upright path
Your feet must struggle; in such bold ascent
The pastoral mountains front you, face to face.
But, courage! for around that boisterous brook
The mountains have all opened out themselves,
And made a hidden valley of their own.
No habitation can be seen; but they
Who journey thither find themselves alone
With a few sheep, with rocks and stones, and kites

That overhead are sailing in the sky.
It is in truth an utter solitude;
Nor should I have made mention of this Dell
But for one object which you might pass by,
Might see and notice not. Beside the brook
Appears a straggling heap of unhewn stones!
And to that simple object appertains
A story—unenriched with strange events,
Yet not unfit, I deem, for the fireside,
Or for the summer shade. It was the first
Of those domestic tales that spake to me
Of Shepherds, dwellers in the valleys, men
Whom I already loved;—not verily
For their own sakes, but for the fields and hills
Where was their occupation and abode.
And hence this Tale, while I was yet a Boy
Careless of books, yet having felt the power
Of Nature, by the gentle agency
Of natural objects, led me on to feel
For passions that were not my own, and think
(At random and imperfectly indeed)
On man, the heart of man, and human life.
Therefore, although it be a history
Homely and rude, I will relate the same
For the delight of a few natural hearts;
And, with yet fonder feeling, for the sake
Of youthful Poets, who among these hills
Will be my second self when I am gone.

      Upon the forest-side in Grasmere Vale
There dwelt a Shepherd, Michael was his name;
An old man, stout of heart, and strong of limb.
His bodily frame had been from youth to age
Of an unusual strength: his mind was keen,

Intense, and frugal, apt for all affairs,
And in his shepherd's calling he was prompt
And watchful more than ordinary men.
Hence had he learned the meaning of all winds,
Of blasts of every tone; and, oftentimes,
When others heeded not, He heard the South
Make subterraneous music, like the noise
Of bagpipers on distant Highland hills.
The Shepherd, at such warning, of his flock
Bethought him, and he to himself would say,
"The winds are now devising work for me!"
And, truly, at all times, the storm, that drives
The traveller to a shelter, summoned him
Up to the mountains: he had been alone
Amid the heart of many thousand mists,
That came to him, and left him, on the heights.
So lived he till his eightieth year was past.
And grossly that man errs, who should suppose
That the green valleys, and the streams and rocks,
Were things indifferent to the Shepherd's thoughts.
Fields, where with cheerful spirits he had breathed
The common air; hills, which with vigorous step
He had so often climbed; which had impressed
So many incidents upon his mind
Of hardship, skill or courage, joy or fear;
Which, like a book, preserved the memory
Of the dumb animals, whom he had saved,
Had fed or sheltered, linking to such acts
The certainty of honourable gain;
Those fields, those hills—what could they less? had laid
Strong hold on his affections, were to him
A pleasurable feeling of blind love,
The pleasure which there is in life itself.

His days had not been passed in singleness.
His Helpmate was a comely matron, old—
Though younger than himself full twenty years.
She was a woman of a stirring life,
Whose heart was in her house: two wheels she had
Of antique form; this large, for spinning wool;
That small, for flax; and if one wheel had rest,
It was because the other was at work.
The Pair had but one inmate in their house,
An only Child, who had been born to them
When Michael, telling o'er his years, began
To deem that he was old,—in shepherd's phrase,
With one foot in the grave. This only Son,
With two brave sheep-dogs tried in many a storm,
The one of an inestimable worth,
Made all their household. I may truly say,
That they were as a proverb in the vale
For endless industry. When day was gone,
And from their occupations out of doors
The Son and Father were come home, even then,
Their labour did not cease; unless when all
Turned to the cleanly supper-board, and there,
Each with a mess of pottage and skimmed milk,
Sat round the basket piled with oaten cakes,
And their plain home-made cheese. Yet when the
    meal
Was ended, Luke (for so the Son was named)
And his old Father both betook themselves
To such convenient work as might employ
Their hands by the fire-side; perhaps to card
Wool for the Housewife's spindle, or repair
Some injury done to sickle, flail, or scythe,
Or other implement of house or field.

Down from the ceiling, by the chimney's edge,
That in our ancient uncouth country style
With huge and black projection overbrowed
Large space beneath, as duly as the light
Of day grew dim the Housewife hung a lamp;
An aged utensil, which had performed
Service beyond all others of its kind.
Early at evening did it burn—and late,
Surviving comrade of uncounted hours,
Which, going by from year to year, had found,
And left the couple neither gay perhaps
Nor cheerful, yet with objects and with hopes,
Living a life of eager industry.
And now, when Luke had reached his eighteenth
        year,
There by the light of this old lamp they sate,
Father and Son, while far into the night
The Housewife plied her own peculiar work,
Making the cottage through the silent hours
Murmur as with the sound of summer flies.
This light was famous in its neighbourhood,
And was a public symbol of the life
That thrifty Pair had lived. For, as it chanced,
Their cottage on a plot of rising ground
Stood single, with large prospect, north and south,
High into Easedale, up to Dunmail-Raise,
And westward to the village near the lake;
And from this constant light, so regular
And so far seen, the House itself, by all
Who dwelt within the limits of the vale,
Both old and young, was named THE EVENING
        STAR.

Thus living on through such a length of years,
The Shepherd, if he loved himself, must needs
Have loved his Helpmate; but to Michael's heart

This son of his old age was yet more dear—
Less from instinctive tenderness, the same
Fond spirit that blindly works in the blood of all—
Than that a child, more than all other gifts
That earth can offer to declining man,
Brings hope with it, and forward-looking thoughts,
And stirrings of inquietude, when they
By tendency of nature needs must fail.
Exceeding was the love he bare to him,
His heart and his heart's joy! For oftentimes
Old Michael, while he was a babe in arms,
Had done him female service, not alone
For pastime and delight, as is the use
Of fathers, but with patient mind enforced
To acts of tenderness; and he had rocked
His cradle, as with a woman's gentle hand.
And, in a later time, ere yet the Boy
Had put on boy's attire, did Michael love,
Albeit of a stern unbending mind,
To have the Young-one in his sight, when he
Wrought in the field, or on his shepherd's stool
Sate with a fettered sheep before him stretched
Under the large old oak, that near his door
Stood single, and, from matchless depth of shade,
Chosen for the Shearer's covert from the sun,
Thence in our rustic dialect was called
The CLIPPING TREE, a name which yet it bears.
There, while they two were sitting in the shade,
With others round them, earnest all and blithe,
Would Michael exercise his heart with looks
Of fond correction and reproof bestowed
Upon the Child, if he disturbed the sheep
By catching at their legs, or with his shouts
Scared them, while they lay still beneath the shears.

And when by Heaven's good grace the boy
    grew up
A healthy Lad, and carried in his cheek
Two steady roses that were five years old;
Then Michael from a winter coppice cut
With his own hand a sapling, which he hooped
With iron, making it throughout in all
Due requisites a perfect shepherd's staff,
And gave it to the Boy; wherewith equipt
He as a watchman oftentimes was placed
At gate or gap, to stem or turn the flock;
And, to his office prematurely called,
There stood the urchin, as you will divine,
Something between a hindrance and a help;
And for this cause not always, I believe,
Receiving from his Father hire of praise;
Though nought was left undone which staff,
    or voice,
Or looks, or threatening gestures, could perform.

But soon as Luke, full ten years old, could stand
Against the mountain blasts; and to the heights,
Not fearing toil, nor length of weary ways,
He with his Father daily went, and they
Were as companions, why should I relate
That objects which the Shepherd loved before
Were dearer now? that from the Boy there came
Feelings and emanations—things which were
Light to the sun and music to the wind;
And that the old Man's heart seemed born again?

Thus in his Father's sight the Boy grew up:
And now, when he had reached his eighteenth year,
He was his comfort and his daily hope.

While in this sort the simple household lived
From day to day, to Michael's ear there came
Distressful tidings. Long before the time
Of which I speak, the Shepherd had been bound
In surety for his brother's son, a man
Of an industrious life, and ample means;
But unforeseen misfortunes suddenly
Had prest upon him; and old Michael now
Was summoned to discharge the forfeiture,
A grievous penalty, but little less
Than half his substance. This unlooked-for claim,
At the first hearing, for a moment took
More hope out of his life than he supposed
That any old man ever could have lost.
As soon as he had armed himself with strength
To look his trouble in the face, it seemed
The Shepherd's sole resource to sell at once
A portion of his patrimonial fields.
Such was his first resolve; he thought again,
And his heart failed him. "Isabel," said he,
Two evenings after he had heard the news,
"I have been toiling more than seventy years,
And in the open sunshine of God's love
Have we all lived; yet if these fields of ours
Should pass into a stranger's hand, I think
That I could not lie quiet in my grave.
Our lot is a hard lot; the sun himself
Has scarcely been more diligent than I;
And I have lived to be a fool at last
To my own family. An evil man
That was, and made an evil choice, if he
Were false to us; and if he were not false,
There are ten thousand to whom loss like this

Had been no sorrow. I forgive him;—but
'Twere better to be dumb than to talk thus.

"When I began, my purpose was to speak
Of remedies and of a cheerful hope.
Our Luke shall leave us, Isabel; the land
Shall not go from us, and it shall be free;
He shall possess it, free as is the wind
That passes over it. We have, thou know'st,
Another kinsman—he will be our friend
In this distress. He is a prosperous man,
Thriving in trade—and Luke to him shall go,
And with his kinsman's help and his own thrift
He quickly will repair this loss, and then
He may return to us. If here he stay,
What can be done? Where every one is poor,
What can be gained?"

    At this the old Man paused,
And Isabel sat silent, for her mind
Was busy, looking back into past times.
There's Richard Bateman, thought she to herself,
He was a parish-boy—at the church-door
They made a gathering for him, shillings, pence
And halfpennies, wherewith the neighbours bought
A basket, which they filled with pedlar's wares;
And, with this basket on his arm, the lad
Went up to London, found a master there,
Who, out of many, chose the trusty boy
To go and overlook his merchandise
Beyond the seas; where he grew wondrous rich,
And left estates and monies to the poor,
And, at his birth-place, built a chapel floored
With marble, which he sent from foreign lands.
These thoughts, and many others of like sort,

Passed quickly through the mind of Isabel,
And her face brightened. The old Man was glad,
And thus resumed:—"Well, Isabel! this scheme
These two days, has been meat and drink to me.
Far more than we have lost is left us yet.
—We have enough—I wish indeed that I
Were younger;—but this hope is a good hope.
Make ready Luke's best garments, of the best
Buy for him more, and let us send him forth
To-morrow, or the next day, or to-night:
—If he *could* go, the Boy should go to-night."

Here Michael ceased, and to the fields went forth
With a light heart. The Housewife for five days
Was restless morn and night, and all day long
Wrought on with her best fingers to prepare
Things needful for the journey of her son.
But Isabel was glad when Sunday came
To stop her in her work: for, when she lay
By Michael's side, she through the last two nights
Heard him, how he was troubled in his sleep:
And when they rose at morning she could see
That all his hopes were gone. That day at noon
She said to Luke, while they two by themselves
Were sitting at the door, "Thou must not go:
We have no other Child but thee to lose,
None to remember—do not go away,
For if thou leave thy Father he will die."
The Youth made answer with a jocund voice;
And Isabel, when she had told her fears,
Recovered heart. That evening her best fare
Did she bring forth, and all together sat
Like happy people round a Christmas fire.

With daylight Isabel resumed her work;
And all the ensuing week the house appeared
As cheerful as a grove in Spring: at length

The expected letter from their kinsman came,
With kind assurances that he would do
His utmost for the welfare of the Boy;
To which, requests were added, that forthwith
He might be sent to him. Ten times or more
The letter was read over; Isabel
Went forth to show it to the neighbours round;
Nor was there at that time on English land
A prouder heart than Luke's. When Isabel
Had to her house returned, the old Man said,
"He shall depart to-morrow." To this word
The Housewife answered, talking much of things
Which, if at such short notice he should go,
Would surely be forgotten. But at length
She gave consent, and Michael was at ease.

Near the tumultuous brook of Green-head Ghyll,
In that deep valley, Michael had designed
To build a Sheep-fold; and, before he heard
The tidings of his melancholy loss,
For this same purpose he had gathered up
A heap of stones, which by the streamlet's edge
Lay thrown together, ready for the work.
With Luke that evening thitherward he walked:
And soon as they had reached the place he stopped,
And thus the old Man spake to him:—"My Son,
To-morrow thou wilt leave me: with full heart
I look upon thee, for thou art the same
That wert a promise to me ere thy birth,
And all thy life hast been my daily joy.
I will relate to thee some little part
Of our two histories; 'twill do thee good
When thou art from me, even if I should touch
On things thou canst not know of.—After thou
First cam'st into the world—as oft befals

To new-born infants—thou didst sleep away
Two days, and blessings from thy Father's tongue
Then fell upon thee. Day by day passed on,
And still I loved thee with increasing love.
Never to living ear came sweeter sounds
Than when I heard thee by our own fire-side
First uttering, without words, a natural tune;
While thou, a feeding babe, didst in thy joy
Sing at thy Mother's breast. Month followed month,
And in the open fields my life was passed
And on the mountains; else I think that thou
Hadst been brought up upon thy Father's knees.
But we were playmates, Luke: among these hills,
As well thou knowest, in us the old and young
Have played together, nor with me didst thou
Lack any pleasure which a boy can know."
Luke had a manly heart; but at these words
He sobbed aloud. The old Man gra sped his hand,
And said, "Nay, do not take it so—I see
That these are things of which I need not speak.
—Even to the utmost I have been to thee
A kind and a good Father: and herein
I but repay a gift which I myself
Received at others' hands; for, though now old
Beyond the common life of man, I still
Remember them who loved me in my youth.
Both of them sleep together: here they lived,
As all their Forefathers had done; and when
At length their time was come, they were not loth
To give their bodies to the family mould.
I wished that thou should'st live the life they lived:
But, 'tis a long time to look back, my Son,
And see so little gain from threescore years.
These fields were burthened when they came to me;
Till I was forty years of age, not more

Than half of my inheritance was mine.
I toiled and toiled; God blessed me in my work,
And till these three weeks past the land was free.
—It looks as if it never could endure
Another Master. Heaven forgive me, Luke,
If I judge ill for thee, but it seems good
That thou should'st go,"

At this the old Man paused;
Then, pointing to the stones near which they stood,
Thus, after a short silence, he resumed:
"This was a work for us; and now, my Son,
It is a work for me. But, lay one stone—
Here, lay it for me, Luke, with thine own hands.
Nay, Boy, be of good hope;—we both may live
To see a better day. At eighty-four
I still am strong and hale;—do thou thy part;
I will do mine.—I will begin again
With many tasks that were resigned to thee:
Up to the heights, and in among the storms,
Will I without thee go again, and do
All works which I was wont to do alone,
Before I knew thy face.—Heaven bless thee, Boy!
Thy heart these two weeks has been beating fast
With many hopes; it should be so—yes—yes—

I knew that thou could'st never have a wish
To leave me, Luke: thou hast been bound to me
Only by links of love: when thou art gone,
What will be left to us!—But, I forget
My purposes. Lay now the corner-stone,
As I requested; and hereafter, Luke,
When thou art gone away, should evil men
Be thy companions, think of me, my Son,
And of this moment; hither turn thy thoughts,

And God will strengthen thee: amid all fear
And all temptation, Luke, I pray that thou
May'st bear in mind the life thy Fathers lived,
Who, being innocent, did for that cause
Bestir them in good deeds. Now, fare thee well—
When thou return'st, thou in this place wilt see
A work which is not here: a covenant
'Twill be between us; but, whatever fate
Befal thee, I shall love thee to the last,
And bear thy memory with me to the grave."

The Shepherd ended here; and Luke stooped down,
And, as his Father had requested, laid
The first stone of the Sheep-fold. At the sight
The old Man's grief broke from him; to his heart
He pressed his Son, he kissed him and wept;
And to the house together they returned.
—Hushed was that House in peace, or seeming
     peace,
Ere the night fell:—with morrow's dawn the Boy
Began his journey, and when he had reached
The public way, he put on a bold face;
And all the neighbours, as he passed their doors,
Came forth with wishes and with farewell
     prayers,
That followed him till he was out of sight.

A good report did from their Kinsman come,
Of Luke and his well doing: and the Boy
Wrote loving letters, full of wondrous news,
Which, as the Housewife phrased it, were
     throughout
"The prettiest letters that were ever seen."
Both parents read them with rejoicing hearts.
So, many months passed on: and once again
The Shepherd went about his daily work

With confident and cheerful thoughts; and now
Sometimes when he could find a leisure hour
He to that valley took his way, and there
Wrought at the Sheep-fold. Meantime Luke began
To slacken in his duty; and, at length,
He in the dissolute city gave himself
To evil courses: ignominy and shame
Fell on him, so that he was driven at last
To seek a hiding-place beyond the seas.

There is a comfort in the strength of love;
'Twill make a thing endurable, which else
Would overset the brain, or break the heart:
I have conversed with more than one who well
Remember the old Man, and what he was
Years after he had heard this heavy news.
His bodily frame had been from youth to age
Of an unusual strength. Among the rocks
He went, and still looked up to sun and cloud,
And listened to the wind; and, as before,
Performed all kinds of labour for his sheep,
And for the land, his small inheritance.
And to that hollow dell from time to time
Did he repair, to build the Fold of which
His flock had need. 'Tis not forgotten yet
The pity which was then in every heart
For the old Man—and 'tis believed by all
That many and many a day he thither went,
And never lifted up a single stone.

There, by the Sheep-fold, sometimes was he seen
Sitting alone, or with his faithful Dog,
Then old, beside him, lying at his feet.
The length of full seven years, from time to time,
He at the building of this Sheep-fold wrought,
And left the work unfinished when he died.

Three years, or little more, did Isabel
Survive her Husband: at her death the estate
Was sold, and went into a stranger's hand.
The Cottage which was named the EVENING
    STAR
Is gone—the ploughshare has been through the
    ground
On which it stood; great changes have been wrought
In all the neighbourhood:—yet the oak is left
That grew beside their door; and the remains
Of the unfinished Sheep-fold may be seen
Beside the boisterous brook of Green-head Ghyll.

The Idle Shepherd-Boys

The valley rings with mirth and joy;
Among the hills the echoes play
A never never ending song,
To welcome in the May.
The magpie chatters with delight;
The mountain raven's youngling brood
Have left the mother and the nest;
And they go rambling east and west
In search of their own food;
Or through the glittering vapours dart
In very wantonness of heart.

Beneath a rock, upon the grass,
Two boys are sitting in the sun;
Their work, if any work they have,
Is out of mind—or done.
On pipes of sycamore they play
The fragments of a Christmas hymn;
Or with that plant which in our dale

We call stag-horn, or fox's tail,
Their rusty hats they trim:
And thus, as happy as the day,
Those Shepherds wear the time away.

Along the river's stony marge
The sand-lark chants a joyous song;
The thrush is busy in the wood,
And carols loud and strong.
A thousand lambs are on the rocks,
All newly born! both earth and sky
Keep jubilee, and more than all,
Those boys with their green coronal;
They never hear the cry,
That plaintive cry! which up the hill
Comes from the depth of Dungeon-Ghyll.

Said Walter, leaping from the ground,
"Down to the stump of yon old yew
We'll for our whistles run a race."
—Away the shepherds flew;
They leapt—they ran—and when they came
Right opposite to Dungeon-Ghyll,
Seeing that he should lose the prize,
"Stop!" to his comrade Walter cries—
James stopped with no good will:
Said Walter then, exulting; "Here
You'll find a task for half a year.

"Cross, if you dare, where I shall cross—
Come on, and tread where I shall tread."
The other took him at his word,
And followed as he led.
It was a spot which you may see
If ever you to Langdale go;
Into a chasm a mighty block

Hath fallen, and made a bridge of rock:
The gulf is deep below;
And, in a basin black and small,
Receives a lofty waterfall.

With staff in hand across the cleft
The challenger pursued his march;
And now, all eyes and feet, hath gained
The middle of the arch.
When list! he hears a piteous moan—
Again!—his heart within him dies—
His pulse is stopped, his breath is lost,
He totters, pallid as a ghost,
And, looking down, espies
A lamb, that in the pool is pent
Within that black and frightful rent.

The lamb had slipped into the stream,
And safe without a bruise or wound
The cataract had borne him down
Into the gulf profound.
His dam had seen him when he fell,
She saw him down the torrent borne;
And, while with all a mother's love
She from the lofty rocks above
Sent forth a cry forlorn,
The lamb, still swimming round and round,
Made answer to that plaintive sound.

When he had learnt what thing it was,
That sent this rueful cry; I ween
The Boy recovered heart, and told
The sight which he had seen.
Both gladly now deferred their task;
Nor was there wanting other aid—
A Poet, one who loves the brooks
Far better than the sages' books,

By chance had thither strayed;
And there the helpless lamb he found
By those huge rocks encompassed round.

He drew it from the troubled pool,
And brought it forth into the light:
The Shepherds met him with his charge,
An unexpected sight!
Into their arms the lamb they took,
Whose life and limbs the flood had spared;
Then up the steep ascent they hied,
And placed him at his mother's side;
And gently did the Bard
Those idle Shepherd-boys upbraid,
And bade them better mind their trade.

The Waterfall and the Eglantine

I

"Begone, thou fond presumptuous Elf,"
Exclaimed an angry Voice,
"Nor dare to thrust thy foolish self
Between me and my choice!"
A small Cascade fresh swoln with snows
Thus threatened a poor Briar-rose,
That, all bespattered with his foam,
And dancing high and dancing low,
Was living, as a child might know,
In an unhappy home.

II

"Dost thou presume my course to block?
Off, off! or, puny Thing!
I'll hurl thee headlong with the rock
To which thy fibres cling."

The Flood was tyrannous and strong;
The patient Briar suffered long,
Nor did he utter groan or sigh,
Hoping the danger would be past;
But, seeing no relief, at last,
He ventured to reply.

III

"Ah!" said the Briar, "blame me not;
Why should we dwell in strife?
We who in this sequestered spot
Once lived a happy life!
You stirred me on my rocky bed—
What pleasure through my veins you spread
The summer long, from day to day,
My leaves you freshened and bedewed;
Nor was it common gratitude
That did your cares repay.

IV

"When spring came on with bud and bell,
Among these rocks did I
Before you hang my wreaths to tell
That gentle days were nigh!
And in the sultry summer hours,
I sheltered you with leaves and flowers;
And in my leaves—now shed and gone,
The linnet lodged, and for us two
Chanted his pretty songs, when you
Had little voice or none.

V

"But now proud thoughts are in your breast—
What grief is mine you see,
Ah! would you think, even yet how blest
Together we might be!
Though of both leaf and flower bereft,
Some ornaments to me are left—
Rich store of scarlet hips is mine,
With which I, in my humble way,
Would deck you many a winter day,
A happy Eglantine!"

VI

What more he said I cannot tell,
The Torrent down the rocky dell
Came thundering loud and fast;
I listened, nor aught else could hear;
The Briar quaked—and much I fear
Those accents were his last.

Song for the Wandering Jew

Though the torrents from their fountains
Roar down many a craggy steep,
Yet they find among the mountains
Resting-places calm and deep.

Clouds that love through air to hasten,
Ere the storm its fury stills,
Helmet-like themselves will fasten
On the heads of towering hills.

What, if through the frozen centre
Of the Alps the Chamois bound,
Yet he has a home to enter
In some nook of chosen ground:

And the Sea-horse, though the ocean
Yield him no domestic cave,
Slumbers without sense of motion,
Couched upon the rocking wave.

If on windy days the Raven
Gambol like a dancing skiff,
Not the less she loves her haven
In the bosom of the cliff.

The fleet Ostrich, till day closes,
Vagrant over desert sands,
Brooding on her eggs reposes
When chill night that care demands.

Day and night my toils redouble,
Never nearer to the goal;
Night and day, I feel the trouble
Of the Wanderer in my soul.

Lines Written with a Slate Pencil upon a Stone

Stranger! this hillock of mis-shapen stones
Is not a Ruin spared or made by time,
Nor, as perchance thou rashly deem'st, the Cairn
Of some old British Chief: 'tis nothing more
Than the rude embryo of a little Dome
Or Pleasure-house, once destined to be built
Among the birch-trees of this rocky isle.
But, as it chanced, Sir William having learned
That from the shore a full-grown man might wade,

And make himself a freeman of this spot
At any hour he chose, the prudent Knight
Desisted, and the quarry and the mound
Are monuments of his unfinished task.
The block on which these lines are traced,
    perhaps,
Was once selected as the corner-stone
Of that intended Pile, which would have been
Some quaint odd plaything of elaborate skill,
So that, I guess, the linnet and the thrush,
And other little builders who dwell here,
Had wondered at the work. But blame him not,
For old Sir William was a gentle Knight,
Bred in this vale, to which he appertained
With all his ancestry. Then peace to him,
And for the outrage which he had devised
Entire forgiveness!—But if thou art one
On fire with thy impatience to become
An inmate of these mountains,—if, disturbed
By beautiful conceptions, thou hast hewn
Out of the quiet rock the elements
Of thy trim Mansion destined soon to blaze
In snow white splendour,—think again; and,
    taught
By old Sir William and his quarry, leave
Thy fragments to the bramble and the rose;
There let the vernal slow warm sun himself,
And let the redbreast hop from stone to stone.

To a Butterfly

Stay near me—do not take thy flight!
A little longer stay in sight!
Much converse do I find in thee,
Historian of my infancy!
Float near me; do not yet depart!
Dead times revive in thee:
Thou bring'st, gay creature as thou art!
A solemn image to my heart,
My father's family!

Oh! pleasant, pleasant were the days,
The time, when, in our childish plays,
My sister Emmeline and I
Together chased the butterfly!
A very hunter did I rush
Upon the prey:—with leaps and springs
I followed on from brake to bush;
But she, God love her! feared to brush
The dust from off its wings.

The Redbreast Chasing the Butterfly

Art thou the bird whom Man loves best,
The pious bird with the scarlet breast,
    Our little English Robin;
The bird that comes about our doors
When Autumn-winds are sobbing?
Art thou the Peter of Norway Boors?
    Their Thomas in Finland,
    And Russia far inland?
The bird, that by some name or other
All men who know thee call their brother,
The darling of children and men?

Could Father Adam open his eyes
And see this sight beneath the skies,
He'd wish to close them again.
—If the Butterfly knew but his friend,
Hither his flight he would bend;
And find his way to me,
Under the branches of the tree:
In and out, he darts about;
Can this be the bird, to man so good,
That, after their bewildering,
Covered with leaves the little children,
     So painfully in the wood?

What ailed thee, Robin, that thou could'st pursue
     A beautiful creature,
That is gentle by nature?
Beneath the summer sky
From flower to flower let him fly;
'Tis all that he wishes to do.
The cheerer Thou of our in-door sadness,
He is the friend of our summer gladness:
What hinders, then, that ye should be
Playmates in the sunny weather,
And fly about in the air together!
His beautiful wings in crimson are drest,
A crimson as bright as thine own:
Would'st thou be happy in thy nest,
O pious Bird! whom man loves best,
Love him, or leave him alone!

It is a Beauteous Evening, Calm and Free

It is a beauteous evening, calm and free,
The holy time is quiet as a Nun
Breathless with adoration; the broad sun
Is sinking down in its tranquility;
The gentleness of heaven broods o'er the Sea;
Listen! the mighty Being is awake,
And doth with his eternal motion make
A sound like thunder—everlastingly.
Dear child! dear Girl! that walkest with me here,
If thou appear untouched by solemn thought,
Thy nature is not therefore less divine:
Thou liest in Abraham's bosom all the year;
And worshipp'st at the Temple's inner shrine,
God being with thee when we know it not.

Composed After a Journey Across the Hambleton Hills

Dark and more dark the shades of evening fell;
The wished-for point was reached—but at an hour
When little could be gained from that rich dower
Of prospect, whereof many thousands tell.
Yet did the glowing west with marvellous power
Salute us; there stood Indian citadel,
Temple of Greece, and minster with its tower
Substantially expressed—a place for bell
Or clock to toll from! Many a tempting isle,
With groves that never were imagined, lay
'Mid seas how steadfast! objects all for the eye
Of silent rapture; but we felt the while
We should forget them; they are of the sky,
And from our earthly memory fade away.

The Sun Has Long Been Set

The sun has long been set,
The stars are out by twos and threes,
The little birds are piping yet
Among the bushes and trees;
There's a cuckoo, and one or two thrushes,
And a far-off wind that rushes,
And a sound of water that gushes,
And the cuckoo's sovereign cry
Fills all the hollow of the sky.

Who would go "parading"
In London, "and masquerading,"
On such a night of June
With that beautiful soft half-moon,
And all these innocent blisses?
On such a night as this is!

Yew-Trees

There is a Yew-tree, pride of Lorton Vale,
Which to this day stands single, in the midst
Of its own darkness, as it stood of yore:
Not loth to furnish weapons for the bands
Of Umfraville or Percy ere they marched
To Scotland's heaths; or those that crossed the sea
And drew their sounding bows at Azincour,
Perhaps at earlier Crecy, or Poictiers.
Of vast circumference and gloom profound
This solitary Tree! a living thing
Produced too slowly ever to decay;
Of form and aspect too magnificent
To be destroyed. But worthier still of note
Are those fraternal Four of Borrowdale,

Joined in one solemn and capacious grove;
Huge trunks! and each particular trunk a growth
Of intertwisted fibres serpentine
Up-coiling, and inveterately convolved;
Nor uninformed with Phantasy, and looks
That threaten the profane;—a pillared shade,
Upon whose grassless floor of red-brown hue,
By sheddings from the pining umbrage tinged
Perennially—beneath whose sable roof
Of boughs, as if for festal purpose, decked
With unrejoicing berries—ghostly Shapes
May meet at noontide; Fear and trembling Hope,
Silence and Foresight; Death the Skeleton
And Time the Shadow;—there to celebrate,
As in a natural temple scattered o'er
With altars undisturbed of mossy stone,
United worship; or in mute repose
To lie, and listen to the mountain flood
Murmuring from Glaramara's inmost caves.

Dorothy Wordsworth

From *Recollections of a Tour Made in Scotland,*
A.D. 1803

First Week.

William and I parted from Mary on Sunday afternoon,
August 14th, 1803; and William, Coleridge, and I left
Keswick on Monday morning, the 15th, at twenty minutes
after eleven o'clock. The day was very hot; we walked up
the hills, and along all the rough road, which made our
walking half the day's journey. Travelled under the foot
of Carrock, a mountain covered with stones on the lower
part; above, it is very rocky, but sheep pasture there; we saw
several where there seemed to be no grass to tempt them.
Passed the foot of Grisdale and Mosedale, both pastoral

valleys, narrow, and soon terminating in the mountains—green, with scattered trees and houses, and each a beautiful stream. At Grisdale our horse backed upon a steep bank where the road was not fenced, just above a pretty mill at the foot of the valley; and we had a second threatening of a disaster in crossing a narrow bridge between the two dales; but this was not the fault of either man or horse. Slept at Mr. Younghusband's public-house, Hesket Newmarket. In the evening walked to Caldbeck Falls, a delicious spot in which to breathe out a summer's day—limestone rocks, hanging trees, pools, and waterbreaks—caves and caldrons which have been honoured with fairy names, and no doubt continue in the fancy of the neighbourhood to resound with fairy revels.

Tuesday, August 16th.—Passed Rose Castle upon the Caldew, an ancient building of red stone with sloping gardens, an ivied gateway, velvet lawns, old garden walls, trim flower-borders with stately and luxuriant flowers. We walked up to the house and stood some minutes watching the swallows that flew about restlessly, and flung their shadows upon the sunbright walls of the old building; the shadows glanced and twinkled, interchanged and crossed each other, expanded and shrunk up, appeared and disappeared every instant; as I observed to William and Coleridge, seeming more like living things than the birds themselves. Dined at Carlisle; the town in a bustle with the assizes; so many strange faces known in former times and recognised, that it half seemed as if I ought to know them all, and, together with the noise, the fine ladies, etc., they put me into confusion. This day Hatfield was condemned I stood at the door of the gaoler's house, where he was; William entered the house, and Coleridge saw him; I fell into conversation with a debtor, who told me in a dry way that he was 'far over-learned,' and another man observed to William that we might learn from Hatfield's fate 'not to meddle with pen and ink.' We gave a shilling to my companion, whom we found out to be a friend of the family, a fellow-sailor with my brother John 'in Captain Wordsworth's ship.' Walked upon the city walls, which are broken down in places and crumbling away, and most disgusting from filth. The city and neighbourhood of Carlisle disappointed me; the banks of the river quite flat, and, though the holms are rich, there is not much beauty in the vale from the want of trees—at least to the eye of a person coming from England, and, I scarcely know how, but to me the holms had not a natural look; there was something townish in their appearance, a dulness in their strong deep green. To Longtown—not very interesting, except from the long views over the flat country; the road rough, chiefly newly mended. Reached Longtown after sunset, a town of brick houses belonging chiefly to the Graham family. Being in the form of a cross and not long, it had been better called Crosstown. There are several shops, and it is not a very small place; but I could not meet with a silver thimble, and bought a halfpenny brass one. Slept at the Graham's Arms, a large inn. Here, as everywhere else, the people seemed utterly insensible of the enormity of Hatfield's offences; the ostler told William that he was quite a gentleman, paid every one genteelly, etc. etc. He and 'Mary' had walked together to Gretna Green; a heavy rain came on when they were there; a returned chaise happened to pass, and the driver would have taken them up; but 'Mr. Hope's' carriage was to be sent for; he did not choose to accept the chaise-driver's offer.

Wednesday, August 17th.—Left Longtown after breakfast. About half-a-mile from the town a guide-post and two roads, to Edinburgh and Glasgow; we took the left-hand road, to Glasgow. Here saw a specimen of the luxuriance of the heath-plant, as it grows in Scotland; it was in the enclosed plantations—perhaps sheltered by them. These plantations appeared to be not well grown for their age; the trees were stunted. Afterwards the road, treeless, over a peat-moss common—the Solway Moss; here and there an earth-built hut with its peat stack, a scanty growing willow hedge round the kailgarth, perhaps the cow pasturing near,—a little lass watching it,—the dreary waste cheered by the endless singing of larks.

We enter Scotland by crossing the river Sark; on the Scotch side of the bridge the ground is unenclosed pasturage; it was very green, and scattered over with that yellow flowered plant which we call grunsel; the hills heave and swell prettily enough; cattle feeding; a few corn fields near the river. At the top of the hill opposite is Springfield, a village built by Sir William Maxwell—a dull uniformity in the houses, as is usual when all built at one time, or belonging to one individual, each just big enough for two people to live in, and in which a family, large or small as it may happen, is crammed. There the marriages are performed. Further on, though almost contiguous, is Gretna Green, upon a hill and among trees. This sounds well, but it is a dreary place; the stone houses dirty and miserable, with broken windows. There is a pleasant view from the churchyard over Solway Firth to the Cumberland mountains. Dined at Annan. On our left as we travelled along appeared the Solway Firth and the mountains beyond, but the near country dreary. Those houses by the roadside which are built of stone are comfortless and dirty; but we peeped into a clay 'biggin' that was very 'canny,' and I daresay will be as warm as a swallow's nest in winter. The town of Annan made me think of France and Germany; many of the houses large and gloomy, the size of them outrunning the comforts. One thing which was like Germany pleased me: the shopkeepers express their calling by some device or painting; bread-bakers have biscuits, loaves, cakes painted on their window-shutters; blacksmiths horses' shoes, iron tools, etc. etc.; and so on through all trades.

Reached Dumfries at about nine o'clock—market-day; met crowds of people on the road, and every one had a smile for us and our car.... The inn was a large house, and tolerably comfortable; Mr. Rogers and his sister, whom we had seen at our own cottage at Grasmere a few days before, had arrived there that same afternoon on their way to the Highlands; but we did not see them till the next morning, and only for about a quarter of an hour.

Thursday, August 18th.—Went to the churchyard where Burns is buried. A bookseller accompanied us. He showed us the outside of Burns's house, where he had lived the last three years of his life, and where he died. It has a mean appearance, and is in a bye situation, whitewashed; dirty about the doors, as almost all Scotch houses are; flowering plants in the windows.

Went on to visit his grave. He lies at a corner of the churchyard, and his second son, Francis Wallace, beside him. There is no stone to mark the spot; but a hundred guineas have been collected, to be expended on some sort of monument. 'There,' said the bookseller, pointing to a pompous monument, 'there lies Mr. Such-a-one'—I have forgotten his name,—'a remarkably clever man; he was an attorney, and hardly ever lost a cause he undertook. Burns made many a lampoon upon him, and there they rest, as you see.' We looked at the grave with melancholy and painful reflections, repeating to each other his own verses:—

'Is there a man whose judgment clear
Can others teach the course to steer,
Yet runs himself life's mad career
　　Wild as the wave?—
Here let him pause, and through a tea
　　Survey this grave.
The Poor Inhabitant below
Was quick to learn, and wise to know,
And keenly felt the friendly glow
　　And softer flame;
But thoughtless follies laid him low,
　　And stain'd his name.'

The churchyard is full of grave-stones and expensive monuments in all sorts of fantastic shapes—obelisk-wise, pillar-wise, etc. In speaking of Gretna Green, I forgot to mention that we visited the churchyard. The church is like a huge house; indeed, so are all the churches, with a steeple, not a square tower or spire,—a sort of thing more like a glass-house chimney than a Church of England steeple; grave-stones in abundance, few verses, yet there were some—no texts. Over the graves of married women the maiden name instead of that of the husband, 'spouse' instead of 'wife,' and the place of abode preceded by 'in' instead of 'of.' When our guide had left us, we turned again to Burns's house. Mrs. Burns was gone to spend some time by the sea-shore with her children. We spoke to the servant-maid at the door, who invited us forward, and we sate down in the parlour. The walls were coloured with a blue wash; on one side of the fire was a mahogany desk, opposite to the window a clock, and over the desk a print from the 'Cotter's Saturday Night,' which Burns mentions in one of his letters having received as a present. The house was cleanly and neat in the inside, the stairs of stone, scoured white, the kitchen on the right side of the passage, the parlour on the left. In the room above the parlour the Poet died, and his son after him in the same room. The servant told us she had lived five years with Mrs. Burns, who was now in great sorrow for the death of 'Wallace.' She said that Mrs. Burns's youngest son was at Christ's Hospital.

We were glad to leave Dumfries, which is no agreeable place to them who do not love the bustle of a town that seems to be rising up to wealth. We could think of little else but poor Burns, and his moving about on that unpoetic ground. In our road to Brownhill, the next stage, we passed Ellisland at a little distance on our right, his farmhouse. We might there have had more pleasure in looking round, if we had been nearer to the spot; but there is no thought surviving in connexion with Burns's daily life that is not heart-depressing. Travelled through the vale of Nith, here little like a vale, it is so broad, with irregular hills rising up on each side, in outline resembling the old-fashioned valances of a bed. There is a great deal of arable land; the corn ripe; trees here and there—plantations, clumps, coppices, and a newness in everything. So much of the gorse and broom rooted out that you wonder why it is not all gone, and yet there seems to be almost as much gorse and broom as corn; and they grow one among another you know not how. Crossed the Nith; the vale becomes narrow, and very pleasant; cornfields, green hills, clay cottages; the river's bed rocky, with woody banks. Left the Nith about a mile and a half, and reached Brownhill, a lonely inn, where we slept. The view from the windows was pleasing, though some travellers might have been disposed to quarrel with it for its general nakedness; yet there was abundance of corn. It is an open country—open, yet all over hills. At a little distance were many cottages among trees, that looked very pretty. Brownhill is about seven or eight miles from Ellisland. I fancied to myself, while I was sitting in the parlour, that Burns might have caroused there, for most likely his rounds extended so far, and this thought gave a melancholy interest to the smoky walls. It was as pretty a room as a thoroughly dirty one could be—a square parlour painted green, but so covered over with smoke and dirt that it looked not unlike green seen through black gauze. There were three windows, looking three ways, a buffet ornamented with tea-cups, a superfine largeish looking-glass with gilt ornaments spreading far and wide, the glass spotted with dirt, some ordinary alehouse pictures, and above the chimney-piece a print in a much better style—as William guessed, taken from a painting by Sir Joshua Reynolds—of some lady of quality, in the character of Euphrosyne. 'Ay,' said the servant girl, seeing that we looked at it, 'there's many travellers would give a deal for that, it's more admired than any in the house.' We could not but smile; for the rest were such as may be found in the basket of any Italian image and picture hawker.

William and I walked out after dinner; Coleridge was not well, and slept upon the carriage cushions. We made our way to the cottages among the little hills and knots of wood, and then saw what a delightful country this part of Scotland might be made by planting forest trees. The ground all over heaves and swells like a sea; but for miles there are neither trees nor hedgerows, only 'mound' fences and tracts; or slips of corn, potatoes, clover—with hay between, and barren land; but near the cottages many hills and hillocks covered with wood. We passed some fine trees, and paused under the shade of one close by an old mansion that seemed from its neglected state to be inhabited by farmers. But I must say that many of the 'gentlemen's' houses which we have passed in Scotland have an air of neglect, and even of desolation. It was a beech, in the full glory of complete and perfect growth, very tall, with one thick stem mounting to a considerable height, which was split into four 'thighs,' as Coleridge afterwards called them, each in size a fine tree. Passed another mansion, now tenanted by a schoolmaster; many boys playing upon the lawn. I cannot take leave of the country which we passed through to-day, without mentioning that we saw the Cumberland mountains within half a mile of Ellisland, Burns's house, the last view we had of them. Drayton has prettily described the connexion which this neighbourhood has with ours when he makes Skiddaw say—

'Scurfell from the sky,
That Anadale doth crown, with a most amorous eye,
Salutes me every day, or at my pride looks grim,
Oft threatning me with clouds, as I oft threatning
    him.'

These lines recurred to William's memory, and we talked of Burns, and of the prospect he must have had, perhaps from his own door, of Skiddaw and his companions, indulging ourselves in the fancy that we might have been personally known to each other, and he have looked upon those objects with more pleasure for our sakes. We talked of Coleridge's children and family, then at the foot of Skiddaw, and our own new-born John a few miles behind it; while the grave of Burns's son, which we had just seen by the side of his father, and some stories heard at Dumfries respecting the dangers his surviving children were exposed to, filled us with melancholy concern, which had a kind of connexion with ourselves. In recollection of this, William long afterwards wrote the following Address to the sons of the ill-fated poet:—

Ye now are panting up life's hill,
'Tis twilight time of good and ill,
And more than common strength and skill
    Must ye display,
If ye would give the better will
    Its lawful sway.
Strong-bodied if ye be to bear
Intemperance with less harm, beware,
But if your Father's wit ye share,
    Then, then indeed,
Ye Sons of Burns, for watchful care
    There will be need.
For honest men delight will take
To shew you favour for his sake,
Will flatter you, and Fool and Rake
    Your steps pursue,
And of your Father's name will make
    A snare for you.
Let no mean hope your souls enslave,
Be independent, generous, brave;
Your Father such example gave,
    And such revere,
But be admonished by his grave,
    And think and fear.

Friday, August 19th.—Open country for a considerable way.
Passed through the village of Thornhill, built by the Duke
of Queensberry; the 'brother-houses' so small that they
might have been built to stamp a character of insolent pride
on his own huge mansion of Drumlanrigg, which is full
in view on the opposite side of the Nith. This mansion is
indeed very large; but to us it appeared like a gathering
together of little things. The roof is broken into a hundred
pieces, cupolas, etc., in the shape of casters, conjuror's

balls, cups, and the like. The situation would be noble if the woods had been left standing; but they have been cut down not long ago, and the hills above and below the house are quite bare. About a mile and a half from Drumlanrigg is a turnpike gate at the top of a hill. We left our car with the man, and turned aside into a field where we looked down upon the Nith, which runs far below in a deep and rocky channel; the banks woody; the view pleasant down the river towards Thornhill, an open country—corn fields, pastures, and scattered trees. Returned to the turnpike house, a cold spot upon a common, black cattle feeding close to the door. Our road led us down the hill to the side of the Nith, and we travelled along its banks for some miles. Here were clay cottages perhaps every half or quarter of a mile. The bed of the stream rough with rocks; banks irregular, now woody, now bare; here a patch of broom, there of corn, then of pasturage; and hills green or heathy above. We were to have given our horse meal and water at a public-house in one of the hamlets we passed through, but missed the house, for, as is common in Scotland, it was without a sign-board. Travelled on, still beside the Nith, till we came to a turnpike house, which stood rather high on the hill-side, and from the door we looked a long way up and down the river. The air coldish, the wind strong.

We asked the turnpike man to let us have some meal and water. He had no meal, but luckily we had part of a feed of corn brought from Keswick, and he procured some hay at a neighbouring house. In the meantime I went into the house, where was an old man with a grey plaid over his shoulders, reading a newspaper. On the shelf lay a volume of the Scotch Encyclopaedia, a History of England, and some other books. The old man was a caller by the way. The man of the house came back, and we began to talk. He was very intelligent; had travelled all over England,

Scotland, and Ireland as a gentleman's servant, and now lived alone in that lonesome place. He said he was tired of his bargain, for he feared he should lose by it. And he had indeed a troublesome office, for coal-carts without number were passing by, and the drivers seemed to do their utmost to cheat him. There is always something peculiar in the house of a man living alone. This was but half-furnished, yet nothing seemed wanting for his comfort, though a female who had travelled half as far would have needed fifty other things. He had no other meat or drink in the house but oat bread and cheese—the cheese was made with the addition of seeds—and some skimmed milk. He gave us of his bread and cheese, and milk, which proved to be sour.

We had yet ten or eleven miles to travel, and no food with us. William lay under the wind in a corn-field below the house, being not well enough to partake of the milk and bread. Coleridge gave our host a pamphlet, 'The Crisis of the Sugar Colonies;' he was well acquainted with Burns's poems. There was a politeness and a manly freedom in this man's manners which pleased me very much. He told us that he had served a gentleman, a captain in the army—he did not know who he was, for none of his relations had ever come to see him, but he used to receive many letters—that he had lived near Dumfries till they would let him stay no longer, he made such havoc with the game; his whole delight from morning till night, and the long year through, was in field sports; he would be on his feet the worst days in winter, and wade through snow up to the middle after his game. If he had company he was in tortures till they were gone; he would then throw off his coat and put on an old jacket not worth half-a-crown. He drank his bottle of wine every day, and two if he had better sport than usual. Ladies sometimes came to stay with his wife, and he often carried them out in an Irish jaunting-car, and if they vexed him he would choose the dirtiest roads possible, and spoil their clothes by jumping in and out of the car, and treading upon them. 'But for all that'—and so he ended all—'he was a good fellow, and a clever fellow, and he liked him well.' He would have ten or a dozen hares in the larder at once, he half maintained his family with game, and he himself was very fond of eating of the spoil—unusual with true heart-and-soul sportsmen.

The man gave us an account of his farm where he had lived, which was so cheap and pleasant that we thought we should have liked to have had it ourselves. Soon after leaving the turnpike house we turned up a hill to the right, the road for a little way very steep, bare hills, with sheep.

After ascending a little while we heard the murmur of a stream far below us, and saw it flowing downwards on our left, towards the Nith, and before us, between steep green hills, coming along a winding valley. The simplicity of the prospect impressed us very much. There was a single cottage by the brook side; the dell was not heathy, but it was impossible not to think of Peter Bell's Highland Girl.

We now felt indeed that we were in Scotland; there was a natural peculiarity in this place. In the scenes of the Nith it had not been the same as England, but yet not simple, naked Scotland. The road led us down the hill, and now there was no room in the vale but for the river and the road; we had sometimes the stream to the right, sometimes to the left. The hills were pastoral, but we did not see many sheep; green smooth turf on the left, no ferns. On the right the heath-plant grew in abundance, of the most exquisite colour; it covered a whole hillside, or it was in streams and patches. We travelled along the vale without appearing to ascend for some miles; all the reaches were beautiful, in exquisite proportion, the hills seeming very high from being so near to us. It might have seemed a valley which nature had kept to herself for pensive thoughts and tender feelings, but that we were reminded at every turning of the road of something beyond by the coal-carts which were travelling towards us. Though these carts broke in upon the tranquillity of the glen, they added much to the picturesque effect of the different views, which indeed wanted nothing, though perfectly bare, houseless, and treeless.

After some time our road took us upwards towards the end of the valley. Now the steeps were heathy all around. Just as we began to climb the hill we saw three boys who came down the cleft of a brow on our left; one carried a fishing-rod, and the hats of all were braided with honey-suckles; they ran after one another as wanton as the wind. I cannot express what a character of beauty those few honeysuckles in the hats of the three boys gave to the place: what bower could they have come from? We walked up the hill, met two well-dressed travellers, the woman barefoot. Our little lads before they had gone far were joined by some half-dozen of their companions, all without shoes and stockings. They told us they lived at Wanlockhead, the village above, pointing to the top of the hill; they went to school and learned Latin, Virgil, and some of them Greek, Homer, but when Coleridge began to inquire further, off they ran, poor things! I suppose afraid of being examined.

When, after a steep ascent, we had reached the top of the hill, we saw a village about half a mile before us on the side of another hill, which rose up above the spot where we were, after a descent, a sort of valley o d poor and half starved, and was scratching his fingers, which were covered with the itch. He was a miner's son, and lived at Wanlockhead; did not go to school, but this was probably on account of his youth. I mention him because he seemed to be a proof that there was poverty and wretchedness among these people, though we saw no other symptom of it; and afterwards we met scores of the inhabitants of this same village. Our road turned to the right, and we saw, at the distance of less than a mile, a tall upright building of grey stone, with several men standing upon the roof, as if they were looking out over battlements. It stood beyond the village, upon higher ground, as if presiding over it,—a kind of enchanter's castle, which it might have been, a place where Don Quixote would have gloried in. When we drew nearer we saw, coming out of the side of the building, a large machine or lever, in appearance like a great forge-hammer, as we supposed for raising water out of the mines. It heaved upwards once in half a minute with a slow motion, and seemed to rest to take breath at the bottom, its motion being accompanied with a sound between a groan and 'jike.' There would have been something in this object very striking in any place, as it was impossible not to invest the machine with some faculty of intellect; it seemed to have made the first step from brute matter to life and purpose, showing its progress by great power. William made a remark to this effect, and Coleridge observed that it was like a giant with one idea. At all events, the object produced a striking effect in that place, where everything was in unison with it—particularly the building itself, which was turret-shaped, and with the figures upon it resembled much one of the fortresses in the wooden cuts of Bunyan's 'Holy War.'

After ascending a considerable way we began to descend again; and now we met a team of horses dragging an immense tree to the lead mines, to repair or add to the building, and presently after we came to a cart, with another large tree, and one horse left in it, right in the middle of the highway. We were a little out of humour, thinking we must wait till the team came back. There were men and boys without number all staring at us; after a little consultation they set their shoulders to the cart, and with a good heave all at once they moved it, and we passed along. These people were decently dressed, and their manners decent; there was no hooting or impudent laughter. Leadhills, another mining village, was the place of our destination for the night; and soon after we had passed the cart we came in sight of it. This village and the mines belong to Lord Hopetoun; it has more stone houses than Wanlockhead, one large old mansion, and a considerable number of old trees—beeches, I believe. The trees told of the coldness of the climate; they were more brown than green—far browner than the ripe grass of the little hay-garths. Here, as at Wanlockhead, were haycocks, hay-stacks, potato-beds, and kail-garths in every possible variety of shape, but, I suppose from the irregularity of the ground, it looked far less artificial—indeed, I should think that a painter might make several beautiful pictures in this village. It straggles down both sides of a mountain glen. As I have said, there is a large mansion. There is also a stone building that looks like a school, and the houses are single, or in clusters, or rows as it may chance.

We passed a decent-looking inn, the Hopetoun Arms; but the house of Mrs. Otto, a widow, had been recommended to us with high encomiums. We did not then understand Scotch inns, and were not quite satisfied at first with our accommodations, but all things were smoothed over by degrees; we had a fire lighted in our dirty parlour, tea came after a reasonable waiting; and the fire with the gentle aid of twilight, burnished up the room into cheerful comfort. Coleridge was weary; but William and I walked out after tea. We talked with one of the miners, who informed us that the building which we had supposed to be a school was a library belonging to the village. He said they had got a book into it a few weeks ago, which had cost thirty pounds, and that they had all sorts of books. 'What! have you Shakespeare?' 'Yes, we have that,' and we found, on further inquiry, that they had a large library, of long standing, that Lord Hopetoun had subscribed liberally to it, and that gentlemen who came with him were in the habit of making larger or smaller donations. Each man who had the benefit of it paid a small sum monthly—I think about fourpence.

The man we talked with spoke much of the comfort and quiet in which they lived one among another; he made use of a noticeable expression, saying that they were 'very peaceable people considering they lived so much underground;'—wages were about thirty pounds a year; they had land for potatoes, warm houses, plenty of coals, and only six hours' work each day, so that they had leisure for reading if they chose. He said the place was healthy, that the inhabitants lived to a great age; and indeed we saw no appearance of ill-health in their countenances; but it is not common for people working in lead mines to be healthy; and I have since heard that it is *not* a healthy place. However this may be, they are unwilling to allow it; for the landlady the next morning, when I said to her 'You have a cold climate,' replied, 'Ay, but it is *varra halesome.*' We inquired of the man respecting the large mansion; he told us that it was built, as we might see, in the form of an H, and belonged to the Hopetouns, and they took their title from thence, and that part of it was used as a chapel. We went close to it, and were a good deal amused with the building itself, standing forth in bold contradiction of the story which I daresay every man of Leadhills tells, and every man believes, that it is in the shape of an H; it is but half an H, and one must be very accommodating to allow it even so much, for the legs are far too short.

We visited the burying-ground, a plot of land not very small, crowded with graves, and upright grave-stones, overlooking the village and the dell. It was now the closing in of evening. Women and children were gathering in the linen for the night, which was bleaching by the burn-side;—the graves overgrown with grass, such as, by industrious culture, had been raised up about the houses; but there were bunches of heather here and there, and with the blue-bells that grew among the grass the small plot of ground had a beautiful and wild appearance.

William left me, and I went to a shop to purchase some thread; the woman had none that suited me; but she would send a '*wee* lad' to the other shop. In the meantime I sat with the mother, and was much pleased with her manner and conversation. She had an excellent fire, and her cottage, though very small, looked comfortable and cleanly; but remember I saw it only by firelight. She confirmed what the man had told us of the quiet manner in which they lived; and indeed her house and fireside seemed to need nothing to make it a cheerful happy spot, but health and good humour. There was a bookishness, a certain formality in this woman's language, which was very remarkable. She had a dark complexion, dark eyes, and wore a very white cap, much over her face, which gave her the look of a French woman, and indeed afterwards the women on the roads frequently reminded us of French women, partly from the extremely white caps of the elder women, and still more perhaps from a certain gaiety and party-coloured appearance in their dress in general. White bed-gowns are very common, and you rarely meet a young girl with either hat or cap; they buckle up their hair often in a graceful manner.

I returned to the inn, and went into the kitchen to speak with the landlady; she had made a hundred hesitations when I told her we wanted three beds. At last she confessed she *had* three beds, and showed me into a parlour which looked damp and cold, but she assured me in a tone that showed she was unwilling to be questioned further, that all *her* beds were well aired. I sat a while by the kitchen fire with the landlady, and began to talk to her; but, much as I had heard in her praise—for the shopkeeper had told me she was a varra discreet woman—I cannot say that her manners pleased me much. But her servant made amends, for she was as pleasant and cheerful a lass as was ever seen; and when we asked her to do anything, she answered, 'Oh yes,' with a merry smile, and almost ran to get us what we wanted. She was about sixteen years old: wore shoes and stockings, and had her hair tucked up with a comb. The servant at Brownhill was a coarse-looking wench, barefoot and barelegged. I examined the kitchen round about; it was crowded with furniture, drawers, cupboards, dish-covers, pictures, pans, and pots, arranged without order, except that the plates were on shelves, and the dish-covers hung in rows; these were very clean, but floors, passages, staircase, everything else dirty. There were two beds in recesses in the wall; above one of them I noticed a shelf with some books:—it made me think of Chaucer's Clerke of Oxenforde:—

> 'Liever had he at his bed's head
> Twenty books clothed in black and red.'

They were baking oat-bread, which they cut into quarters, and half-baked over the fire, and half-toasted before it. There was a suspiciousness about Mrs. Otto, almost like ill-nature; she was very jealous of any inquiries that might appear to be made with the faintest idea of a comparison between Leadhills and any other place, except the advantage was evidently on the side of Leadhills. We had nice honey to breakfast. When ready to depart, we learned that we might have seen the library, which we had not thought of till it was too late, and we were very sorry to go away without seeing it.

Saturday, August 20th. — Left Leadhills at nine o'clock, regretting much that we could not stay another day, that we might have made more minute inquiries respecting the manner of living of the miners, and been able to form an estimate, from our own observation, of the degree of knowledge, health, and comfort that there was among them. The air was keen and cold; we might have supposed it to be three months later in the season and two hours earlier in the day. The landlady had not lighted us a fire; so I was obliged to get myself toasted in the kitchen, and when we set off I put on both grey cloak and spencer.

Our road carried us down the valley, and we soon lost sight of Leadhills, for the valley made a turn almost immediately, and we saw two miles, perhaps, before us; the glen sloped somewhat rapidly—heathy, bare, no hut or house. Passed by a shepherd, who was sitting upon the ground, reading, with the book on his knee, screened from the wind by his plaid, while a flock of sheep were feeding near him among the rushes and coarse grass—for, as we descended we came among lands where grass grew with the heather. Travelled through several reaches of the glen, which somewhat resembled the valley of Menock on the other side of Wanlockhead; but it was not near so beautiful; the forms of the mountains did not melt so exquisitely into each other, and there was a coldness, and, if I may so speak, a want of simplicity in the surface of the earth; the heather was poor, not covering a whole hillside; not in luxuriant streams and beds interveined with rich verdure; but patchy and stunted, with here and there coarse grass and rushes. But we soon came in sight of a spot that impressed us very much. At the lower end of this new reach of the vale was a decayed tree, beside a decayed cottage, the vale spreading out into a level area which was one large field, without fence and without division, of a dull yellow colour; the vale seemed to partake of the desolation of the cottage, and to participate in its decay. And yet the spot was in its nature so dreary that one would rather have wondered how it ever came to be tenanted by man, than lament that it was left to waste and solitude. Yet the encircling hills were so exquisitely formed that it was impossible to conceive anything more lovely than this place would have been if the valley and hill-sides had been interspersed with trees, cottages, green fields, and hedgerows. But all was desolate; the one large field which filled up the area of the valley appeared, as I have said, in decay, and seemed to retain the memory of its connexion with man in some way analogous to the ruined building; for it was as much of a field as Mr. King's best pasture scattered over with his fattest cattle.

We went on, looking before us, the place losing nothing of its hold upon our minds, when we discovered a woman sitting right in the middle of the field, alone, wrapped up in a grey cloak or plaid. She sat motionless all the time we looked at her, which might be nearly half an hour. We could not conceive why she sat there, for there were neither sheep nor cattle in the field; her appearance was very melancholy. In the meantime our road carried us nearer to the cottage, though we were crossing over the hill to the left, leaving the valley below us, and we perceived that a part of the building was inhabited, and that what we had supposed to be *one* blasted tree was eight trees, four of which were entirely blasted; the others partly so, and round about the place was a little potato and cabbage garth, fenced with earth. No doubt, that woman had been an inhabitant of the cottage. However this might be, there was so much obscurity and uncertainty about her, and her figure agreed so well with the desolation of the place, that we were indebted to the chance of her being there for some of the most interesting feelings that we had ever had from natural objects connected with man in dreary solitariness.

We had been advised to go along the *new* road, which would have carried us down the vale; but we met some travellers who recommended us to climb the hill, and go by the village of Crawfordjohn as being much nearer. We had a long hill, and after having reached the top, steep and bad roads, so we continued to walk for a considerable way. The air was cold and clear—the sky blue. We walked cheerfully along in the sunshine, each of us alone, only William had the charge of the horse and car, so he sometimes took a ride, which did but poorly recompense him for the trouble of driving. I never travelled with more cheerful spirits than this day. Our road was along the side of a high moor. I can always walk over a moor with a light foot; I seem to be drawn more closely to nature in such places than anywhere else; or rather I feel more strongly the power of nature over me, and am better satisfied with myself for being able to find enjoyment in what unfortunately to many persons is either dismal or insipid. This moor, however, was more than commonly interesting; we could see a long way, and on every side of us were larger or smaller tracts of cultivated land. Some were extensive farms, yet in so large a waste they did but look small, with farm-houses, barns, etc., others like little cottages, with enough to feed a cow, and supply the family with vegetables. In looking at these farms we had always one feeling. Why did the plough stop there? Why might not they as well have carried it twice as far? There were no hedgerows near the farms, and very few trees. As we were passing along, we saw an old man, the first we had seen in a Highland bonnet, walking with a staff at a very slow pace by the edge of one of the moorland cornfields; he wore a grey plaid, and a dog was by his side. There was a scriptural solemnity in this man's figure, a sober simplicity which was most impressive. Scotland is the country above all others that I have seen, in which a man of imagination may carve out his own pleasures. There are so many *inhabited* solitudes, and the employments of the people are so immediately connected with the places where you find them, and their dresses so simple, so much alike, yet, from their being folding garments, admitting of an endless variety, and falling often so gracefully.

After some time we descended towards a broad vale, passed one farm-house, sheltered by fir trees, with a burn close to it; children playing, linen bleaching. The vale was open pastures and corn-fields unfenced, the land poor. The village of Crawfordjohn on the slope of a hill a long way before us to the left. Asked about our road of a man who was driving a cart; he told us to go through the village, then along some fields, and we should come to a 'herd's house by the burn side.' The highway was right through the vale, unfenced on either side; the people of the village, who were making hay, all stared at us and our carriage. We inquired the road of a middle-aged man, dressed in a shabby black coat, at work in one of the hay fields; he looked like the minister of the place, and when he spoke we felt assured that he was so, for he was not sparing of hard words, which, however, he used with great propriety, and he spoke like one who had been accustomed to dictate. Our car wanted mending in the wheel, and we asked him if there was a blacksmith in the village. 'Yes,' he replied, but when we showed him the wheel he told William that he might mend it himself without a blacksmith, and he would put him in the way; so he fetched hammer and nails and gave his directions, which William obeyed, and repaired the damage entirely to his own satisfaction and the priest's, who did not offer to lend any assistance himself; not as if he would not have been willing in case of need; but as if it were more natural for him to dictate, and because he thought it more fit that William should do it himself. He spoke much about the propriety of every man's lending all the assistance in his power to travellers, and with some ostentation or self-praise. Here I observed a honey-suckle and some flowers growing in a garden, the first I had seen in Scotland. It is a pretty cheerful-looking village, but must be very cold in winter; it stands on a hillside, and the vale itself is very high ground, unsheltered by trees.

Left the village behind us, and our road led through arable ground for a considerable way, on which were growing very good crops of corn and potatoes. Our friend accompanied us to show us the way, and Coleridge and he had a scientific conversation concerning the uses and properties of lime and other manures. He seemed to be a well-informed man; somewhat pedantic in his manners; but this might be only the difference between Scotch and English.

Soon after he had parted from us, we came upon a stony, rough road over a black moor; and presently to the 'herd's house by the burn side.' We could hardly cross the burn dry-shod, over which was the only road to the cottage. In England there would have been stepping-stones or a bridge; but the Scotch need not be afraid of wetting their bare feet. The hut had its little kail-garth fenced with earth; there was no other enclosure—but the common, heathy with coarse grass. Travelled along the common for some miles, before we joined the great road from Longtown to Glasgow—saw on the bare hill-sides at a distance, sometimes a solitary farm, now and then a plantation, and one very large wood, with an appearance of richer ground above; but it was so very high we could not think it possible. Having descended considerably, the common was no longer of a peat-mossy brown heath colour, but grass with rushes was its chief produce; there was sometimes a solitary hut, no enclosures except the kail-garth, and sheep pasturing in flocks, with shepherd-boys tending them. I remember one boy in particular; he had no hat on, and only had a grey plaid wrapped about him. It is nothing to describe, but on a bare moor, alone with his sheep, standing, as he did, in utter quietness and silence, there was something uncommonly impressive in his appearance, a solemnity which recalled to our minds the old man in the corn-field. We passed many people who were mowing, or raking the grass of the common; it was little better than rushes; but they did not mow straight forward, only here and there, where it was the best; in such a place hay-cocks had an uncommon appearance to us.

After a long descent we came to some plantations which were not far from Douglas Mill. The country for some time had been growing into cultivation, and now it was a wide vale with large tracts of corn; trees in clumps, no hedgerows, which always make a country look bare and unlovely. For my part, I was better pleased with the desert places we had left behind, though no doubt the inhabitants of this place think it 'a varra bonny spot,' for the Scotch are always pleased with their own abode, be it what it may; and afterwards at Edinburgh, when we were talking with a bookseller of our travels, he observed that it was 'a fine country near Douglas Mill.' Douglas Mill is a single house, a large inn, being one of the regular stages between Longtown and Glasgow, and therefore a fair specimen of the best of the country inns of Scotland. As soon as our car stopped at the door we felt the difference. At an English inn of this size, a waiter, or the master or mistress, would have been at the door immediately, but we remained some time before anybody came; then a barefooted lass made her appearance, but she only looked at us and went away. The mistress, a remarkably handsome woman, showed us into a large parlour; we ordered mutton-chops, and I finished my letter to Mary; writing on the same window-ledge on which William had written to me two years before.

After dinner, William and I sat by a little mill-race in the garden. We had left Leadhills and Wanlockhead far above us, and now were come into a warmer climate; but there was no richness in the face of the country. The shrubs looked cold and poor, and yet there were some very fine trees within a little distance of Douglas Mill, so that the reason, perhaps, why the few low shrubs and trees which were growing in the gardens seemed to be so unluxuriant, might be, that there being no hedgerows, the general appearance of the country was naked, and I could not help seeing the same coldness where, perhaps, it did not exist in itself to any great degree, for the corn crops are abundant, and I should think the soil is not bad. While we were sitting at the door, two of the landlady's children came out; the elder, a boy about six years old, was running away from his little brother, in petticoats; the ostler called out, 'Sandy, tak' your wee brither wi' you;' another voice from the window, 'Sawny, dinna leave your wee brither;' the mother then came, 'Alexander, tak' your wee brother by the hand;' Alexander obeyed, and the two went off in peace together. We were charged eightpence for hay at this inn, another symptom of our being in Scotland. Left Douglas Mill at about three o'clock; travelled through an open corn country, the tracts of corn large and unenclosed. We often passed women or children who were watching a single cow while it fed upon the slips of grass between the corn. William asked a strong woman, about thirty years of age, who looked like the mistress of a family—I suppose moved by some sentiment of compassion for her being so employed,—if the cow would eat the corn if it were left to itself: she smiled at his simplicity. It is indeed a melancholy thing to see a full-grown woman thus waiting, as it were, body and soul devoted to the poor beast; yet even this is better than working in a manufactory the day through.

We came to a moorish tract; saw before us the hills of Loch Lomond, Ben Lomond and another, distinct each by itself. Not far from the roadside were some benches placed in rows in the middle of a large field, with a sort of covered shed like a sentry-box, but much more like those boxes which the Italian puppet-showmen in London use. We guessed that it was a pulpit or tent for preaching, and were told that a sect met there occasionally, who held that toleration was unscriptural, and would have all religions but their own exterminated. I have forgotten what name the man gave to this sect; we could not learn that it differed in any other respect from the Church of Scotland. Travelled for some miles along the open country, which was all without hedgerows, sometimes arable, sometimes moorish, and often whole tracts covered with grunsel. There was one field, which one might have believed had been sown with grunsel, it was so regularly covered with it—a large square field upon a slope, its boundary marked to our eyes only by the termination of the bright yellow; contiguous to it were other fields of the same size and shape, one of clover, the other of potatoes, all equally regular crops. The oddness of this appearance, the grunsel being uncommonly luxuriant, and the field as yellow as gold, made William laugh. Coleridge was melancholy upon it, observing that there was land enough wasted to rear a healthy child.

We left behind us, considerably to the right, a single high mountain; I have forgotten its name; we had had it long in view. Saw before us the river Clyde, its course at right angles to our road, which now made a turn, running parallel with the river; the town of Lanerk in sight long before we came to it. I was somewhat disappointed with the first view of the Clyde: the banks, though swelling and varied, had a poverty in their appearance, chiefly from the want of wood and hedgerows. Crossed the river and ascended towards Lanerk, which stands upon a hill. When we were within about a mile of the town, William parted from Coleridge and me, to go to the celebrated waterfalls. Coleridge did not attempt to drive the horse; but led him all the way. We inquired for the best inn, and were told that the New Inn was the best; but that they had very 'genteel apartments' at the Black Bull, and made less charges, and the Black Bull was at the entrance of the town, so we thought we would stop there, as the horse was obstinate and weary. But when we came to the Black Bull we had no wish to enter the apartments; for it seemed the abode of dirt and poverty, yet it was a large building. The town showed a sort of French face, and would have done much more, had it not been for the true British tinge of coal-smoke; the doors and windows dirty, the shops dull, the women too seemed to be very dirty in their dress. The town itself is not ugly; the houses are of grey stone, the streets not very narrow, and the market-place decent. The New Inn is a handsome old stone building, formerly a gentleman's house. We were conducted into a parlour, where people had been drinking; the tables were unwiped, chairs in disorder, the floor dirty, and the smell of liquors was most offensive. We were tired, however, and rejoiced in our tea.

The evening sun was now sending a glorious light through the street, which ran from west to east; the houses were of a fire red, and the faces of the people as they walked westward were almost like a blacksmith when he is at work by night. I longed to be out, and meet with William, that we might see the Falls before the day was gone. Poor Coleridge was unwell, and could not go. I inquired my road, and a little girl told me she would go with me to the porter's lodge, where I might be admitted. I was grieved to hear that the Falls of the Clyde were shut up in a gentleman's grounds, and to be viewed only by means of lock and key. Much, however, as the pure feeling with which one would desire to visit such places is disturbed by useless, impertinent, or even unnecessary interference with nature, yet when I was there the next morning I seemed to feel it a less disagreeable thing than in smaller and more delicate spots, if I may use the phrase. My guide, a sensible little girl, answered my inquiries very prettily. She was eight years old, read in the 'Collection,' a book which all the Scotch children whom I have questioned read in. I found it was a collection of hymns; she could repeat several of Dr. Watts'. We passed through a great part of the town, then turned down a steep hill, and came in view of a long range of cotton mills, the largest and loftiest I had ever seen; climbed upwards again, our road leading us along the top of the left bank of the river; both banks very steep and richly wooded. The girl left me at the porter's lodge. Having asked after William, I was told that no person had been there, or could enter but by the gate. The night was coming on, therefore I did not venture to go in, as I had no hope of meeting William. I had a delicious walk alone through the wood; the sound of the water was very solemn, and even the cotton mills in the fading light of evening had somewhat of the majesty and stillness of the natural objects. It was nearly dark when I reached the inn. I found Coleridge sitting by a good fire, which always makes an inn room look comfortable. In a few minutes William arrived; he had heard of me at the gate, and followed as quickly as he could, shouting after me. He was pale and exceedingly tired.

After he had left us he had taken a wrong road, and while looking about to set himself right had met with a barefooted boy, who said he would go with him. The little fellow carried him by a wild path to the upper of the Falls, the Boniton Linn, and coming down unexpectedly upon it, he was exceedingly affected by the solemn grandeur of the place. This fall is not much admired or spoken of by travellers; you have never a full, breast view of it; it does not make a complete self-satisfying place, an abode of its own, as a perfect waterfall seems to me to do; but the river, down which you look through a long vista of steep and ruin-like rocks, the roaring of the waterfall, and the solemn evening lights, must have been most impressive. One of the rocks on the near bank, even in broad daylight, as we saw it the next morning, is exactly like the fractured arch of an abbey. With the lights and shadows of evening upon it, the resemblance must have been much more striking.

William's guide was a pretty boy, and he was exceedingly pleased with him. Just as they were quitting the waterfall, William's mind being full of the majesty of the scene, the little fellow pointed to the top of a rock, 'There's a fine slae-bush there.' 'Ay,' said William, 'but there are no slaes upon it,' which was true enough; but I suppose the child remembered the slaes of another summer, though, as he said, he was but 'half seven years old,' namely, six and a half. He conducted William to the other fall, and as they were going along a narrow path, they came to a small cavern, where William lost him, and looking about, saw his pretty figure in a sort of natural niche fitted for a statue, from which the boy jumped out laughing, delighted with the success of his trick. William told us a great deal about him, while he sat by the fire, and of the pleasure of his walk, often repeating, 'I wish you had been with me.' Having no change, he gave the boy sixpence, which was certainly, if he had formed any expectations at all, far beyond them; but he received it with the utmost indifference, without any remark of surprise or pleasure; most likely he did not know how many halfpence he could get for it, and twopence would have pleased him more. My little girl was delighted with the sixpence I gave her, and said she would buy a book with it on Monday morning. What a difference between the manner of living and education of boys and of girls among the lower classes of people in towns! she had never seen the Falls of the Clyde, nor had ever been further than the porter's lodge; the boy, I daresay, knew every hiding-place in every accessible rock, as well as the fine 'slae bushes' and the nut trees.

Second Week.

Sunday, August 21st.—The morning was very hot, a morning to tempt us to linger by the water-side. I wished to have had the day before us, expecting so much from what William had seen; but when we went there, I did not desire to stay longer than till the hour which we had prescribed to ourselves; for it was a rule not to be broken in upon, that the person who conducted us to the Falls was to remain by our side till we chose to depart. We left our inn immediately after breakfast. The lanes were full of people going to church; many of the middle-aged women wore long scarlet cardinals, and were without hats: they brought to my mind the women of Goslar as they used to go to church in their silver or gold caps, with their long cloaks, black or coloured.

The banks of the Clyde from Lanerk to the Falls rise immediately from the river; they are lofty and steep, and covered with wood. The road to the Falls is along the top of one of the banks, and to the left you have a prospect of the open country, corn fields and scattered houses. To the right, over the river, the country spreads out, as it were, into a plain covered over with hills, no one hill much higher than another, but hills all over; there were endless pastures overgrown with broom, and scattered trees, without hedges or fences of any kind, and no distinct footpaths. It was delightful to see the lasses in gay dresses running like cattle among the broom, making their way straight forward towards the river, here and there as it might chance. They waded across the stream, and, when they had reached the top of the opposite bank, sat down by the road-side, about half a mile from the town, to put on their shoes and cotton stockings, which they brought tied up in pocket-handker-chiefs. The porter's lodge is about a mile from Lanerk, and the lady's house—for the whole belongs to a lady, whose name I have forgotten—is upon a hill at a little distance. We walked, after we had entered the private grounds, perhaps two hundred yards along a gravel carriage-road, then came to a little side gate, which opened upon a narrow gravel path under trees, and in a minute and a half, or less, were directly opposite to the great waterfall. I was much affected by the first view of it. The majesty and strength of the water, for I had never before seen so large a cataract, struck me with astonishment, which died away, giving place to more delightful feelings; though there were some buildings that I could have wished had not been there, though at first unnoticed. The chief of them was a neat, white, lady-like house, very near to the waterfall. William and Coleridge however were in a better and perhaps wiser humour, and did not dislike the house; indeed, it was a very nice-looking place, with a moderate-sized garden, leaving the green fields free and open. This house is on the side of the river opposite to the grand house and the pleasure-grounds. The waterfall Cora Linn is composed of two falls, with a sloping space, which *appears* to be about twenty yards between, but is much more. The basin which receives the fall is enclosed by noble rocks, with trees, chiefly hazels, birch, and ash growing out of their sides whenever there is any hold for them; and a magnificent resting-place it is for such a river; I think more grand than the Falls themselves.

After having stayed some time, we returned by the same footpath into the main carriage-road, and soon came upon what William calls an ell-wide gravel walk, from which we had different views of the Linn. We sat upon a bench, placed for the sake of one of these views, whence we looked down upon the waterfall, and over the open country, and saw a ruined tower, called Wallace's Tower, which stands at a very little distance from the fall, and is an interesting object. A lady and gentleman, more expeditious tourists than ourselves, came to the spot; they left us at the seat, and we found them again at another station above the Falls. Coleridge, who is always good-natured enough to enter into conversation with anybody whom he meets in his way, began to talk with the gentleman, who observed that it was a *majestic* waterfall. Coleridge was delighted with the accuracy of the epithet, particularly as he had been settling in his own mind the precise meaning of the words grand, majestic, sublime, etc., and had discussed the subject with William at some length the day before. 'Yes, sir,' says Coleridge, 'it *is* a majestic waterfall.' 'Sublime and beautiful,' replied his friend. Poor Coleridge could make no answer, and, not very desirous to continue the conversation, came to us and related the story, laughing heartily.

The distance from one Linn to the other may be half a mile or more, along the same ell-wide walk. We came to a pleasure-house, of which the little girl had the key; she said it was called the Fog-house, because it was lined with 'fog,' namely moss. On the outside it resembled some of the huts in the prints belonging to Captain Cook's Voyages, and within was like a hay-stack scooped out. It was circular, with a dome-like roof, a seat all round fixed to the wall, and a table in the middle,—seat, wall, roof and table all covered with moss in the neatest manner possible. It was as snug as a bird's nest; I wish we had such a one at the top of our orchard, only a great deal smaller. We afterwards found that huts of the same kind were common in the pleasure-grounds of Scotland; but we never saw any that were so beautifully wrought as this. It had, however, little else to recommend it, the situation being chosen without judgment; there was no prospect from it, nor was it a place of seclusion and retirement, for it stood close to the ell-wide gravel walk. We wished we could have shoved it about a hundred yards further on, when we arrived at a bench which was also close to the walk, for just below the bench, the walk elbowing out into a circle, there was a beautiful spring of clear water, which we could see rise up continually, at the bottom of a round stone basin full to the brim, the water gushing out at a little outlet and passing away under the walk. A reason was wanted for placing the hut where it is; what a good one would this little spring have furnished for bringing it hither! Along the whole of the path were openings at intervals for views of the river, but, as almost always happens in gentlemen's grounds, they were injudiciously managed; you were prepared for a dead stand—by a parapet, a painted seat, or some other device.

We stayed some time at the Boniton Fall, which has one great advantage over the other falls, that it is at the termination of the pleasure-grounds, and we see no traces of the boundary-line; yet, except under some accidental circumstances, such as a sunset like that of the preceding evening, it is greatly inferior to the Cora Linn. We returned to the inn to dinner. The landlord set the first dish upon the table, as is common in England, and we were well waited upon. This first dish was true Scottish—a boiled sheep's head, with the hair singed off; Coleridge and I ate heartily of it; we had barley broth, in which the sheep's head had been boiled. A party of tourists whom we had met in the pleasure-grounds drove from the door while we were waiting for dinner; I guess they were fresh from England, for they had stuffed the pockets of their carriage with bundles of heather, roots and all, just as if Scotland grew no heather but on the banks of the Clyde. They passed away with their treasure towards Loch Lomond. A party of boys, dressed all alike in blue, very neat, were standing at the chaise-door; we conjectured they were charity scholars; but found on inquiry that they were apprentices to the cotton factory; we were told that they were well instructed in reading and writing. We had seen in the morning a flock of girls dressed in grey coming out of the factory, probably apprentices also.

After dinner set off towards Hamilton, but on foot, for we had to turn aside to the Cartland Rocks, and our car was to meet us on the road. A guide attended us, who might almost in size, and certainly in activity, have been compared with William's companion who hid himself in the niche of the cavern. His method of walking and very quick step soon excited our attention. I could hardly keep up with him; he paddled by our side, just reaching to my shoulder, like a little dog, with his long snout pushed before him—for he had an enormous nose, and walked with his head foremost. I said to him, 'How quick you walk!' he replied, '*That* was *not* quick walking,' and when I asked him what he called so, he said 'Five miles an hour,' and then related in how many hours he had lately walked from Lanerk to Edinburgh, done some errands, and returned to Lanerk—I have forgotten the particulars, but it was a very short time—and added that he had an old father who could walk at the rate of four miles an hour, for twenty-four miles, any day, and had never had an hour's sickness in his life. 'Then,' said

I, 'he has not drunk much strong liquor?' 'Yes, enough to drown him.' From his eager manner of uttering this, I inferred that he himself was a drinker; and the man who met us with the car told William that he gained a great deal of money as an errand-goer, but spent it all in tippling. He had been a shoemaker, but could not bear the confinement on account of a weakness in his chest.

The neighbourhood of Lanerk is exceedingly pleasant; we came to a sort of district of glens or little valleys that cleave the hills, leaving a cheerful, open country above them, with no superior hills, but an undulating surface. Our guide pointed to the situation of the Cartland Crags. We were to cross a narrow valley, and walk down on the other side, and then we should be at the spot; but the little fellow made a sharp turn down a footpath to the left, saying, 'We must have some conversation here.' He paddled on with his small pawing feet till we came right opposite to a gentleman's house on the other side of the valley, when he halted, repeating some words, I have forgotten what, which were taken up by the most distinct echo I ever heard—this is saying little: it was the most distinct echo that it is possible to conceive. It shouted the names of our fireside friends in the very tone in which William and Coleridge spoke; but it seemed to make a joke of me, and I could not help laughing at my own voice; it was so shrill and pert, exactly as if some one had been mimicking it very successfully, with an intention of making me ridiculous. I wished Joanna had been there to laugh, for the echo is an excellent laugher, and would have almost made her believe that it was a true story which William has told of her and the mountains. We turned back, crossed the valley, went through the orchard and plantations belonging to the gentleman's house. By the bye, we observed to our guide that the echo must bring many troublesome visitors to disturb the quiet of the owner of that house. 'Oh no,' said he, 'he glories in much company.' He was a native of that neighbourhood, had made a moderate fortune abroad, purchased an estate, built the house, and raised the plantations; and further, had made a convenient walk through his woods to the Cartland Crags. The house was modest and neat, and though not adorned in the best taste, and though the plantations were of fir, we looked at it with great pleasure, there was such true liberality and kind-heartedness in leaving his orchard path open, and his walks unobstructed by gates. I hope this goodness is not often abused by plunderers of the apple-trees, which were hung with tempting apples close to the path.

At the termination of the little valley, we descended through a wood along a very steep path to a muddy stream running over limestone rocks; turned up to the left along the bed of the stream, and soon we were closed in by rocks on each side. They were very lofty—of limestone, trees starting out of them, high and low, overhanging the stream or shooting up towards the sky. No place of the kind could be more beautiful if the stream had been clear, but it was of a muddy yellow colour; had it been a large river, one might have got the better of the unpleasantness of the muddy water in the grandeur of its roaring, the boiling up of the foam over the rocks, or the obscurity of its pools.

We had been told that the Cartland Crags were better worth going to see than the Falls of the Clyde. I did not think so; but I have seen rocky dells resembling this before, with clear water instead of that muddy stream, and never saw anything like the Falls of the Clyde. It would be a delicious spot to have near one's house; one would linger out many a day in the cool shade of the caverns, and the stream would soothe one by its murmuring; still, being an old friend, one would not love it the less for its homely face. Even we, as we passed along, could not help stopping for a long while to admire the beauty of the lazy foam, for ever in motion, and never moved away, in a still place of the water, covering the whole surface of it with streaks and lines and ever-varying circles. Wild marjoram grew upon the rocks in great perfection and beauty; our guide gave me a bunch, and said he should come hither to collect a store for tea for the winter, and that it was 'varra hale-some:' he drank none else. We walked perhaps half a mile along the bed of the river; but it might *seem* to be much further than it was, owing to the difficulty of the path, and the sharp and many turnings of the glen. Passed two of Wallace's Caves. There is scarce a noted glen in Scotland that has not a cave for Wallace or some other hero. Before we left the river the rocks became less lofty, turned into a wood through which was a convenient path upwards, met the owner of the house and the echo-ground, and thanked him for the pleasure which he had provided for us and other travellers by making such pretty pathways.

It was four o'clock when we reached the place where the car was waiting. We were anxious to be off, as we had fifteen miles to go; but just as we were seating ourselves we found that the cushions were missing. William was forced to go back to the town, a mile at least, and Coleridge and I waited with the car. It rained, and we had some fear that the evening would be wet, but the rain soon ceased, though the sky continued gloomy—an unfortunate circumstance, for we had to travel through a beautiful country, and of that sort which is most set off by sunshine and pleasant weather.

Travelled through the Vale or *Trough* of the Clyde, as it is called, for ten or eleven miles, having the river on our right. We had fine views both up and down the river for the first three or four miles, our road being not close to it, but above its banks, along the open country, which was here occasionally intersected by hedgerows.

Left our car in the road, and turned down a field to the Fall of Stonebyres, another of the falls of the Clyde, which I had not heard spoken of; therefore it gave me the more pleasure. We saw it from the top of the bank of the river at a little distance. It has not the imposing majesty of Cora Linn; but it has the advantage of being left to itself, a grand solitude in the heart of a populous country. We had a prospect above and below it, of cultivated grounds, with hay-stacks, houses, hills; but the river's banks were lonesome, steep, and woody, with rocks near the fall.

A little further on, came more into company with the river; sometimes we were close to it, sometimes above it, but always at no great distance; and now the vale became more interesting and amusing. It is very populous, with villages, hamlets, single cottages, or farm-houses embosomed in orchards, and scattered over with gentlemen's houses, some of them very ugly, tall and obtrusive, others neat and comfortable. We seemed now to have got into a country where poverty and riches were shaking hands together; pears and apples, of which the crop was abundant, hung over the road, often growing in orchards unfenced; or there might be bunches of broom along the road-side in an interrupted line, that looked like a hedge till we came to it and saw the gaps. Bordering on these fruitful orchards perhaps would be a patch, its chief produce being gorse or broom. There was nothing like a moor or common anywhere; but small plots of uncultivated ground were left high and low, among the potatoes, corn, cabbages, which grew intermingled, now among trees, now bare. The Trough of the Clyde is, indeed, a singular and very interesting region; it is somewhat like the upper part of the vale of Nith, but above the Nith is much less cultivated ground—without hedgerows or orchards, or anything that looks like a rich country. We met crowds of people coming from the kirk; the lasses were gaily dressed, often in white gowns, coloured satin bonnets, and coloured silk handkerchiefs, and generally with their shoes and stockings in a bundle hung on their arm. Before we left the river the vale became much less interesting, resembling a poor English country, the fields being large, and unluxuriant hedges.

It had been dark long before we reached Hamilton, and William had some difficulty in driving the tired horse through the town. At the inn they hesitated about being able to give us beds, the house being brim-full—lights at every window. We were rather alarmed for our accommodations during the rest of the tour, supposing the house to be filled with *tourists*; but they were in general only regular travellers for out of the main road from town to town we saw scarcely a carriage, and the inns were empty. There was nothing remarkable in the treatment we met with at this inn, except the lazy impertinence of the waiter. It was a townish place, with a great larder set out; the house throughout dirty.

Monday, August 22d. — Immediately after breakfast walked to the Duke of Hamilton's house to view the picture-gallery, chiefly the famous picture of Daniel in the Lions' Den, by Rubens. It is a large building, without grandeur, a heavy, lumpish mass, after the fashion of the Hopetoun H, only five times the size, and with longer legs, which makes it gloomy. We entered the gate, passed the porter's lodge, where we saw nobody, and stopped at the front door, as William had done two years before with Sir William Rush's family. We were met by a little mean-looking man, shabbily dressed, out of livery, who, we found, was the porter. After scanning us over, he told us that we ought not to have come to that door. We said we were sorry for the mistake, but as one of our party had been there two years before, and was admitted by the same entrance, we had supposed it was the regular way. After many hesitations, and having kept us five minutes waiting in the large hall, while he went to consult with the housekeeper, he informed us that we could not be admitted at that time, the housekeeper being unwell; but that we might return in an hour: he then conducted us through long gloomy passages to an obscure door at the corner of the house. We asked if we might be permitted to walk in the park in the meantime; and he told us that this would not be agreeable to the Duke's family. We returned to the inn discontented enough, but resolved not to waste an hour, if there were anything else in the neighbourhood worth seeing. The waiter told us there was a curious place called Baroncleugh, with gardens cut out in rocks, and we determined to go thither. We had to walk through the town, which may be about as large as Penrith, and perhaps a mile further, along a dusty turnpike road. The morning was hot, sunny, and windy, and we were half tired before we reached the place; but were amply repaid for our trouble.

The general face of the country near Hamilton is much in the ordinary English style; not very hilly, with hedgerows, corn fields, and stone houses. The Clyde is here an open river with low banks, and the country spreads out so wide that there is no appearance of a regular vale. Baroncleugh is in a beautiful deep glen through which runs the river Avon, a stream that falls into the Clyde. The house stands very sweetly in complete retirement; it has its gardens and terraces one above another, with flights of steps between, box-trees and yew-trees cut in fantastic shapes, flower-borders and summer-houses; and, still below, apples and pears were hanging in abundance on the branches of large old trees, which grew intermingled with the natural wood, elms, beeches, etc., even to the water's edge. The whole place is in perfect harmony with the taste of our ancestors, and the yews and hollies are shaven as nicely, and the gravel walks and flower-borders kept in as exact order, as if the spirit of the first architect of the terraces still presided over them. The opposite bank of the river is left in its natural wildness, and nothing was to be seen higher up but the deep dell, its steep banks being covered with fine trees, a beautiful relief or contrast to the garden, which is one of the most elaborate old things ever seen, a little hanging garden of Babylon.

I was sorry to hear that the owner of this sweet place did not live there always. He had built a small thatched house to eke out the old one: it was a neat dwelling, with no false ornaments. We were exceedingly sorry to quit this spot, which is left to nature and past times, and should have liked to have pursued the glen further up; we were told that there was a ruined castle; and the walk itself must be very delightful; but we wished to reach Glasgow in good time, and had to go again to Hamilton House. Returned to the town by a much shorter road, and were very angry with the waiter for not having directed us to it; but he was too great a man to speak three words more than he could help.

We stopped at the proper door of the Duke's house, and seated ourselves humbly upon a bench, waiting the pleasure of the porter, who, after a little time, informed us that we could not be admitted, giving no reason whatever. When we got to the inn, we could just gather from the waiter that it was not usual to refuse admittance to strangers; but that was all: he could not, or would not, help us, so we were obliged to give it up, which mortified us, for I had wished much to see the picture. William vowed that he would write that very night to Lord Archibald Hamilton, stating the whole matter, which he did from Glasgow.

I ought to have mentioned the park, though, as we

were not allowed to walk there, we saw but little of it. It looked pleasant, as all parks with fine trees must be, but, as it seemed to be only a large, nearly level, plain, it could not be a particularly beautiful park, though it borders upon the Clyde, and the Avon runs, I believe, through it, after leaving the solitude of the glen of Baroncleugh.

Quitted Hamilton at about eleven o'clock. There is nothing interesting between Hamilton and Glasgow till we came to Bothwell Castle, a few miles from Hamilton. The country is cultivated, but not rich, the fields large, a perfect contrast to the huddling together of hills and trees, corn and pasture grounds, hay-stacks, cottages, orchards, broom and gorse, but chiefly broom, that had amused us so much the evening before in passing through the Trough of the Clyde. A native of Scotland would not probably be satisfied with the account I have given of the Trough of the Clyde, for it is one of the most celebrated scenes in Scotland. We certainly received less pleasure from it than we had expected; but it was plain that this was chiefly owing to the unfavourable circumstances under which we saw it—a gloomy sky and a cold blighting wind. It is a very beautiful district, yet there, as in all the other scenes of Scotland celebrated for their fertility, we found something which gave us a notion of barrenness, of what was not altogether genial. The new fir and larch plantations, here as in almost every other part of Scotland, contributed not a little to this effect.

Crossed the Clyde not far from Hamilton, and had the river for some miles at a distance from us, on our left; but after having gone, it might be, three miles, we came to a porter's lodge on the left side of the road, where we were to turn to Bothwell Castle, which is in Lord Douglas's grounds. The woman who keeps the gate brought us a book, in which we wrote down our names. Went about half a mile before we came to the pleasure-grounds. Came to a large range of stables, where we were to leave the car; but there was no one to unyoke the horse, so William was obliged to do it himself, a task which he performed very awkwardly, being then new to it. We saw the ruined castle embosomed in trees, passed the house, and soon found ourselves on the edge of a steep brow immediately above and overlooking the course of the river Clyde through a deep hollow between woods and green steeps. We had approached at right angles from the main road to the place over a flat, and had seen nothing before us but a nearly level country terminated by distant slopes, the Clyde hiding himself in his deep bed. It was exceedingly delightful to come thus unexpectedly upon such a beautiful region.

The Castle stands nobly, overlooking the Clyde. When we came up to it I was hurt to see that flower-borders had taken place of the natural overgrowings of the ruin, the scattered stones and wild plants. It is a large and grand pile, of red freestone, harmonizing perfectly with the rocks of the river, from which, no doubt, it has been hewn. When I was a little accustomed to the unnaturalness of a modern garden, I could not help admiring the excessive beauty and luxuriance of some of the plants, particularly the purple-flowered clematis, and a broad-leaved creeping plant without flowers, which scrambled up the castle wall along with the ivy, and spread its vine-like branches so lavishly that it seemed to be in its natural situation, and one could not help thinking that, though not self-planted among the ruins of this country, it must somewhere have its natural abode in such places. If Bothwell Castle had not been close to the Douglas mansion we should have been disgusted with the possessor's miserable conception of 'adorning' such a venerable ruin; but it is so very near to the house that of necessity the pleasure-grounds must have extended beyond it, and perhaps the neatness of a shaven lawn and the complete desolation natural to a ruin might have made an unpleasing contrast; and besides, being within the precincts of the pleasure-grounds, and so very near to the modern mansion of a noble family, it has forfeited in some degree its independent majesty, and becomes a tributary to the mansion; its solitude being interrupted, it has no longer the same command over the mind in sending it back into past times, or excluding the ordinary feelings which we bear about us in daily life. We had then only to regret that the castle and house were so near to each other; and it was impossible not to regret it; for the ruin presides in state over the river, far from city or town, as if it might have had a peculiar privilege to preserve its memorials of past ages and maintain its own character and independence for centuries to come.

We sat upon a bench under the high trees, and had beautiful views of the different reaches of the river above and below. On the opposite bank, which is finely wooded with elms and other trees, are the remains of an ancient priory, built upon a rock: and rock and ruin are so blended together that it is impossible to separate the one from the other. Nothing can be more beautiful than the little remnants of this holy place; elm trees—for we were near enough to distinguish them by their branches—grow out of the walls, and overshadow a small but very elegant window. It can scarcely be conceived what a grace the castle and priory impart to each other; and the river Clyde flows on smooth and unruffled below, seeming to my thoughts more in harmony with the sober and stately images of former times, than if it had roared over a rocky channel, forcing its sound upon the ear. It blended gently with the warbling of the smaller birds and chattering of the larger ones that had made their nests in the ruins. In this fortress the chief of the English nobility were confined after the battle of Bannockburn. If a man is to be a prisoner, he scarcely could have a more pleasant place to solace his captivity; but I thought that for close confinement I should prefer the banks of a lake or the sea-side. The greatest charm of a brook or river is in the liberty to pursue it through its windings; you can then take it in whatever mood you like; silent or noisy, sportive or quiet. The beauties of a brook or river must be sought, and the pleasure is in going in search of them; those of a lake or of the sea come to you of themselves. These rude warriors cared little perhaps about either; and yet if one may judge from the writings of Chaucer and from the old romances, more interesting passions were connected with natural objects in the days of chivalry than now, though going in search of scenery, as it is called, had not then been thought of. I had heard nothing of Bothwell Castle, at least nothing that I remembered, therefore, perhaps, my pleasure was greater, compared with what I received elsewhere, than others might feel [...]

Third Week.

Sunday, August 28th.—We were desirous to have crossed the mountains above Glengyle to Glenfalloch, at the head of Loch Lomond, but it rained so heavily that it was impossible, so the ferryman engaged to row us to the point where Coleridge and I had rested, while William was going on our doubtful adventure. The hostess provided us with tea and sugar for our breakfast; the water was boiled in an iron pan, and dealt out to us in a jug, a proof that she does not often drink tea, though she said she had always tea and sugar in the house. She and the rest of the family breakfasted on curds and whey, as taken out of the pot in which she was making cheese; she insisted upon my taking some also; and her husband joined in with the old story, that it was 'varra halesome.' I thought it exceedingly good, and said to myself that they lived nicely with their cow: she was meat, drink, and company. Before breakfast the house-wife was milking behind the chimney, and I thought I had seldom heard a sweeter fire-side sound; in an evening, sitting over a sleepy, low-burnt fire, it would lull one like the purring of a cat.

When we departed, the good woman shook me cordially by the hand, saying she hoped that if ever we came into Scotland again, we would come and see her. The lake was calm, but it rained so heavily that we could see little. Landed at about ten o'clock, almost wet to the skin, and, with no prospect but of streaming rains, faced the mountain-road to Loch Lomond. We recognised the same objects passed before,—the tarn, the potato-bed, and the cottages with their burnies, which were no longer, as one might say, household streams, but made us only think of the moun-tains and rocks they came from. Indeed, it is not easy to imagine how different everything appeared; the mountains with mists and torrents alive and always changing: but the low grounds where the inhabitants had been at work the day before were melancholy, with here and there a few haycocks and hay scattered about.

Wet as we were, William and I turned out of our path to the Garrison house. A few rooms of it seemed to be inhabited by some wretchedly poor families, and it had all the desolation of a large decayed mansion in the suburbs of a town, abandoned of its proper inhabitants, and become the abode of paupers. In spite of its outside bravery, it was but a poor protection against 'the sword of winter, keen and cold.' We looked at the building through the arch of a broken gateway of the courtyard, in the middle of which it stands. Upon that stormy day it appeared more than desolate; there was something about it even frightful.

When beginning to descend the hill towards Loch Lomond, we overtook two girls, who told us we could not cross the ferry till evening, for the boat was gone with a number of people to church. One of the girls was exceedingly beautiful; and the figures of both of them, in grey plaids falling to their feet, their faces only being uncovered, excited our attention before we spoke to them; but they answered us so sweetly that we were quite delighted, at the same time that they stared at us with an innocent look of wonder. I think I never heard the English language sound more sweetly than from the mouth of the elder of these girls, while she stood at the gate answering our inquiries, her face flushed with the rain; her pronunciation was clear and distinct: without difficulty, yet slow, like that of a foreign speech. They told us we might sit in the ferry-house till the return of the boat, went in with us, and made a good fire as fast as possible to dry our wet clothes. We learnt that the taller was the sister of the ferryman, and had been left in charge with the house for the day, that the other was his wife's sister, and was come with her mother on a visit,— an old woman, who sate in a corner beside the cradle, nursing her little grandchild. We were glad to be housed, with our feet upon a warm hearth-stone; and our attendants were so active and good-humoured that it was pleasant to have to desire them to do anything. The younger was a delicate and unhealthy-looking girl; but there was an uncommon meekness in her countenance, with an air of premature intelligence, which is often seen in sickly young persons. The other made me think of Peter Bell's 'Highland Girl':

'As light and beauteous as a squirrel,
As beauteous and as wild.'

She moved with unusual activity, which was chastened very delicately by a certain hesitation in her looks when she spoke, being able to understand us but imperfectly. They were both exceedingly desirous to get me what I wanted to make me comfortable. I was to have a gown and petticoat of the mistress's; so they turned out her whole wardrobe upon the parlour floor, talking Erse to one another, and laughing all the time. It was long before they could decide which of the gowns I was to have; they chose at last, no doubt thinking that it was the best, a light-coloured sprigged cotton, with long sleeves, and they both laughed while I was putting it on, with the blue linsey petticoat, and one or the other, or both together, helped me to dress, repeating at least half a dozen times, 'You never had on the like of that before.' They held a consultation of several minutes over a pair of coarse woollen stockings, gabbling Erse as fast as their tongues could move, and looked as if uncertain what to do: at last, with great diffidence, they offered them to me, adding, as before, that I had never worn 'the like of them.' When we entered the house we had been not a little glad to see a fowl stewing in barley-broth; and now when the wettest of our clothes were stripped off, began again to recollect that we were hungry, and asked if we could have dinner. 'Oh yes, ye may get that,' the elder replied, pointing to the pan on the fire.

Conceive what a busy house it was—all our wet clothes to be dried, dinner prepared and set out for us four strangers, and a second cooking for the family; add to this, two rough 'callans,' as they called them, boys about eight years old, were playing beside us; the poor baby was fretful all the while; the old woman sang doleful Erse songs, rocking it in its cradle the more violently the more it cried; then there were a dozen cookings of porridge, and it could never be fed without the assistance of all three. The hut was after the Highland fashion, but without anything beautiful except its situation; the floor was rough, and wet with the rain that came in at the door, so that the lasses' bare feet were as wet as if they had been walking through street puddles, in passing from one room to another; the windows were open, as at the other hut; but the kitchen had a bed in it, and was much smaller, and the shape of the house was like that of a common English cottage, without its comfort; yet there was no appearance of poverty— indeed, quite the contrary. The peep out of the open door-place across the lake made some amends for the want of the long roof and elegant rafters of our boatman's cottage, and all the while the waterfall, which we could not see, was roaring at the end of the hut, which seemed to serve as a sounding-board for its noise, so that it was not unlike sitting in a house where a mill is going. The dashing of the waves against the shore could not be distinguished; yet in spite of my knowledge of this I could not help fancying that the tumult and storm came from the lake, and went out several times to see if it was possible to row over in safety.

After long waiting we grew impatient for our dinner; at last the pan was taken off, and carried into the other room; but we had to wait at least another half hour before the ceremony of dishing up was completed; yet with all this bustle and difficulty, the manner in which they, and particularly the elder of the girls, performed everything, was perfectly graceful. We ate a hearty dinner, and had time to get our clothes quite dry before the arrival of the boat. The girls could not say at what time it would be at home; on our asking them if the church was far off they replied, 'Not very far;' and when we asked how far, they said, 'Perhaps about four or five miles.' I believe a Church of England congregation would hold themselves excused for non-attendance three parts of the year, having but half as far to go; but in the lonely parts of Scotland they make little of a journey of nine or ten miles to a preaching. They have not perhaps an opportunity of going more than once in a quarter of a year, and, setting piety aside, have other motives to attend: they hear the news, public and private, and see their friends and neighbours; for, though the people who meet at these times may be gathered together from a circle of twenty miles' diameter, a sort of neighbourly connexion must be so brought about. There is something exceedingly pleasing to my imagination in this gathering together of the inhabitants of these secluded districts—for instance, the borderers of these two large lakes meeting at the deserted garrison which I have described. The manner of their travelling is on foot, on horseback, and in boats across the waters,—young and old, rich and poor, all in their best dress.

If it were not for these Sabbath-day meetings one summer month would be like another summer month, one winter month like another—detached from the goings-on of the world, and solitary throughout; from the time of earliest childhood they will be like landing-places in the memory of a person who has passed his life in these thinly peopled regions; they must generally leave distinct impressions, differing from each other so much as they do in circumstances, in time and place, etc.,—some in the open fields, upon hills, in houses, under large rocks, in storms, and in fine weather.

But I have forgotten the fireside of our hut. After long waiting, the girls, who had been on the look-out, informed us that the boat was coming. I went to the water-side, and saw a cluster of people on the opposite shore; but being yet at a distance, they looked more like soldiers surrounding a carriage than a group of men and women; red and green were the distinguishable colours. We hastened to get ourselves ready as soon as we saw the party approach, but had longer to wait than we expected, the lake being wider than it appears to be. As they drew near we could distinguish men in tartan plaids, women in scarlet cloaks, and green umbrellas by the half-dozen. The landing was as pretty a sight as ever I saw. The bay, which had been so quiet two days before, was all in motion with small waves, while the swoln waterfall roared in our ears. The boat came steadily up, being pressed almost to the water's edge by the weight of its cargo; perhaps twenty people landed, one after another. It did not rain much, but the women held up their umbrellas; they were dressed in all the colours of the rainbow, and, with their scarlet cardinals, the tartan plaids of the men, and Scotch bonnets, made a gay appearance. There was a joyous bustle surrounding the boat, which even imparted something of the same character to the waterfall in its tumult, and the restless grey waves; the young men laughed and shouted, the lasses laughed, and the elder folks seemed to be in a bustle to be away. I remember well with what haste the mistress of the house where we were ran up to seek after her child, and seeing us, how anxiously and kindly she inquired how we had fared, if we had had a good fire, had been well waited upon, etc. etc. All this in three minutes—for the boatman had another party to bring from the other side and hurried us off.

The hospitality we had met with at the two cottages and Mr. Macfarlane's gave us very favourable impressions on this our first entrance into the Highlands, and at this day the innocent merriment of the girls, with their kindness to us, and the beautiful figure and face of the elder, come to my mind whenever I think of the ferry-house and waterfall of Loch Lomond, and I never think of the two girls but the whole image of that romantic spot is before me, a living image, as it will be to my dying day. The following poem was written by William not long after our return from Scotland:—

Sweet Highland Girl, a very shower
Of beauty is thy earthly dower!
Twice seven consenting years have shed
Their utmost bounty on thy head:
And these grey rocks; this household lawn;
These trees, a veil just half withdrawn;
This fall of water, that doth make
A murmur near the silent Lake;
This little Bay, a quiet road
That holds in shelter thy abode;
In truth together ye do seem
Like something fashion'd in a dream;
Such forms as from their covert peep
When earthly cares are laid asleep!
Yet, dream and vision as thou art,
I bless thee with a human heart:
God shield thee to thy latest years!
I neither know thee nor thy peers;
And yet my eyes are filled with tears.

With earnest feeling I shall pray
For thee when I am far away:
For never saw I mien or face,
In which more plainly I could trace
Benignity and home-bred sense
Ripening in perfect innocence.
Here, scattered like a random seed,
Remote from men, thou dost not need
Th' embarrass'd look of shy distress

And maidenly shamefacedness;
Thou wear'st upon thy forehead clear
The freedom of a mountaineer:
A face with gladness overspread!
Sweet smiles, by human-kindness
And seemliness complete, that sways
Thy courtesies, about thee plays;
With no restraint but such as springs
From quick and eager visitings
Of thoughts that lie beyond the reach
Of thy few words of English speech:
A bondage sweetly brook'd, a strife
That gives thy gestures grace and life!
So have I, not unmoved in mind,
Seen birds of tempest-loving kind,
Thus beating up against the wind.

What hand but would a garland cull
For thee, who art so beautiful?
O happy pleasure! here to dwell
Beside thee in some heathy dell;
Adopt your homely ways and dress,
A Shepherd, thou a Shepherdess!
But I could frame a wish for thee
More like a grave reality:
Thou art to me but as a wave
Of the wild sea: and I would have
Some claim upon thee, if I could,
Though but of common neighbourhood.
What joy to hear thee and to see!
Thy elder brother I would be,
Thy father—anything to thee.

Now thanks to Heaven! that of its grace
Hath led me to this lonely place!

Joy have I had; and going hence
I bear away my recompence.
In spots like these it is we prize
Our memory, feel that she hath eyes:
Then why should I be loth to stir?
I feel this place is made for her;
To give new pleasure like the past
Continued long as life shall last.
Nor am I loth, though pleased at heart,
Sweet Highland Girl, from thee to part;
For I, methinks, till I grow old,
As fair before me shall behold
As I do now, the Cabin small,
The Lake, the Bay, the Waterfall,
And thee, the Spirit of them all.

We were rowed over speedily by the assistance of two youths, who went backwards and forwards for their own amusement, helping at the oars, and pulled as if they had strength and spirits to spare for a year to come. We noticed that they had uncommonly fine teeth, and that they and the boatman were very handsome people. Another merry crew took our place in the boat.

We had three miles to walk to Tarbet. It rained, but not heavily; the mountains were not concealed from us by the mists, but appeared larger and more grand; twilight was coming on, and the obscurity under which we saw the objects, with the sounding of the torrents, kept our minds alive and wakeful; all was solitary and huge—sky, water, and mountains mingled together. While we were walking forward, the road leading us over the top of a brow, we stopped suddenly at the sound of a half articulate Gaelic hooting from the field close to us. It came from a little boy, whom we could see on the hill between us and the lake, wrapped up in a grey plaid. He was probably calling home the cattle for the night. His appearance was in the highest degree moving to the imagination: mists were on the hillsides, darkness shutting in upon the huge avenue of mountains, torrents roaring, no house in sight to which the child might belong; his dress, cry, and appearance all different from anything we had been accustomed to. It was a text, as William has since observed to me, containing in itself the whole history of the Highlander's life—his melancholy, his simplicity, his poverty, his superstition, and above all, that visionariness which results from a communion with the unworldliness of nature.

When we reached Tarbet the people of the house were anxious to know how we had fared, particularly the girl who had waited upon us. Our praises of Loch Ketterine made her exceedingly happy, and she ventured to say, of which we had heard not a word before, that it was 'bonnier to *her* fancy than Loch Lomond.' The landlord, who was not at home when we had set off, told us that if he had known of our going he would have recommended us to Mr. Macfarlane's or the other farm-house, adding that they were hospitable people in that vale. Coleridge and I got tea, and William and the drawing-master chose supper; they asked to have a broiled fowl, a dish very common in Scotland, to which the mistress replied, 'Would not a "boiled" one do as well?' They consented, supposing that it would be more easily cooked; but when the fowl made its appearance, to their great disappointment it proved a cold one that had been stewed in the broth at dinner.

Monday, August 29th.—It rained heavily this morning, and, having heard so much of the long rains since we came into Scotland, as well as before, we had no hope that it would be over in less than three weeks at the least, so poor Coleridge, being very unwell, determined to send his clothes to Edinburgh and make the best of his way thither, being afraid to face much wet weather in an open carriage. William and I were unwilling to be confined at Tarbet, so we resolved to go to Arrochar, a mile and a half on the road to Inverary, where there is an inn celebrated as a place of good accommodation for travellers. Coleridge and I set off on foot, and William was to follow with the car, but a heavy shower coming on, Coleridge left me to shelter in a hut and wait for William, while he went on before. This hut was unplastered, and without windows, crowded with beds, uncomfortable, and not in the simplicity of the ferryman's house. A number of good clothes were hanging against the walls, and a green silk umbrella was set up in a corner. I should have been surprised to see an umbrella in such a place before we came into the Highlands; but umbrellas are not so common anywhere as there—a plain proof of the wetness of the climate; even five minutes after this a girl passed us without shoes and stockings, whose gown and petticoat were not worth half a crown, holding an umbrella over her bare head.

We turned at a guide-post, 'To the New Inn,' and, after descending a little, and winding round the bottom of a hill, saw, at a small distance, a white house half hidden by tall trees upon a lawn that slopes down to the side of Loch Long, a sea-loch, which is here very narrow. Right before us, across the lake, was The Cobbler, which appeared to rise directly from the water; but, in fact, it overtopped another hill, being a considerable way behind. The inn looked so much like a gentleman's house that we could hardly believe it was an inn. We drove down the broad gravel walk, and, making a sweep, stopped at the front door, were shown into a large parlour with a fire, and my first thought was,

How comfortable we should be! but Coleridge, who had arrived before us, checked my pleasure: the waiter had shown himself disposed to look coolly upon us, and there had been a hint that we could not have beds;—a party was expected, who had engaged all the beds. We conjectured this might be but a pretence, and ordered dinner in the hope that matters would clear up a little, and we thought they could not have the heart to turn us out in so heavy a rain if it were possible to lodge us. We had a nice dinner, yet would have gladly changed our roasted lamb and pickles, and the gentleman-waiter with his napkin in his pocket, for the more homely fare of the smoky hut at Loch Ketterine, and the good woman's busy attentions, with the certainty of a hospitable shelter at night. After dinner I spoke to the landlord himself, but he was not to be moved: he could not even provide one bed for me, so nothing was to be done but either to return to Tarbet with Coleridge, or that William and I should push on the next stage, to Cairndow. We had an interesting close view from the windows of the room where we sate, looking across the lake, which did not differ in appearance, as we saw it here, from a fresh-water lake. The sloping lawn on which the house stood was prettily scattered over with trees; but we had seen the place to great advantage at our first approach, owing to the mists upon the mountains, which had made them seem exceedingly high, while the strange figures on The Cobbler appeared and disappeared, like living things; but, as the day cleared we were disappointed in what was more like the permanent effect of the scene: the mountains were not so lofty as we had supposed, and the low grounds not so fertile; yet still it is a very interesting, I may say beautiful, place.

The rain ceased entirely, so we resolved to go on to Cairndow, and had the satisfaction of seeing that our landlord had not told us an untruth concerning the expected company; for just before our departure we saw, on the opposite side of the vale, a coach with four horses, another carriage, and two or three men on horseback—a striking procession, as it moved along between the bare mountain and the lake. Twenty years ago, perhaps, such a sight had not been seen here except when the Duke of Argyle, or some other Highland chieftain, might chance to be going with his family to London or Edinburgh. They had to cross a bridge at the head of the lake, which we could not see, so, after disappearing about ten minutes, they drove up to the door—three old ladies, two waiting-women, and store of men-servants. The old ladies were as gaily dressed as bullfinches in spring-time. We heard the next day that they were the renowned Miss Waughs of Carlisle, and that they enjoyed themselves over a game at cards in the evening.

Left Arrochar at about four o'clock in the afternoon. Coleridge accompanied us a little way; we portioned out the contents of our purse before our parting; and, after we had lost sight of him, drove heavily along. Crossed the bridge, and looked to the right, up the vale, which is soon terminated by mountains: it was of a yellow green, with but few trees and few houses; sea-gulls were flying above it. Our road—the same along which the carriages had come—was directly under the mountains on our right hand, and the lake was close to us on our left, the waves breaking among stones overgrown with yellow sea-weed; fishermen's boats, and other larger vessels than are seen on fresh-water lakes were lying at anchor near the opposite shore; seabirds flying overhead; the noise of torrents mingled with the beating of the waves, and misty mountains enclosed the vale;—a melancholy but not a dreary scene. Often have I, in looking over a map of Scotland, followed the intricate windings of one of these sea-lochs, till, pleasing myself with my own imaginations, I have felt a longing, almost painful, to travel among them by land or by water.

This was the first sea-loch we had seen. We came prepared for a new and great delight, and the first impression which William and I received, as we drove rapidly through the rain down the lawn of Arrochar, the objects dancing before us, was even more delightful than we had expected. But, as I have said, when we looked through the window, as the mists disappeared and the objects were seen more distinctly, there was less of sheltered valley-comfort than we had fancied to ourselves, and the mountains were not so grand; and now that we were near to the shore of the lake, and could see that it was not of fresh water, the wreck, the broken sea-shells, and scattered sea-weed gave somewhat of a dull and uncleanly look to the whole lake, and yet the water was clear, and might have appeared as beautiful as that of Loch Lomond, if with the same pure pebbly shore. Perhaps, had we been in a more cheerful mood of mind we might have seen everything with a different eye. The stillness of the mountains, the motion of the waves, the streaming torrents, the sea-birds, the fishing-boats were all melancholy; yet still, occupied as my mind was with other things, I thought of the long windings through which the waters of the sea had come to this inland retreat, visiting the inner solitudes of the mountains, and I could have wished to have mused out a summer's day on the shores of the lake. From the foot of these mountains whither might not a little barque carry one away? Though so far inland, it is but a slip of the great ocean: seamen, fishermen, and shepherds here find a natural home. We did not travel far down the lake, but, turning to the right through an opening of the mountains, entered a glen called Glen Croe.

Our thoughts were full of Coleridge, and when we were enclosed in the narrow dale, with a length of winding road before us, a road that seemed to have insinuated itself into the very heart of the mountains—the brook, the road, bare hills, floating mists, scattered stones, rocks, and herds of black cattle being all that we could see,—I shivered at the thought of his being sickly and alone, travelling from place to place.

The Cobbler, on our right, was pre-eminent above the other hills; the singular rocks on its summit, seen so near, were like ruins—castles or watch-towers. After we had passed one reach of the glen, another opened out, long, narrow, deep, and houseless, with herds of cattle and large stones; but the third reach was softer and more beautiful, as if the mountains had there made a warmer shelter, and there were a more gentle climate. The rocks by the riverside had dwindled away, the mountains were smooth and green, and towards the end, where the glen sloped upwards, it was a cradle-like hollow, and at that point where the slope became a hill, at the very bottom of the curve of the cradle, stood one cottage, with a few fields and beds of potatoes. There was also another house near the roadside, which appeared to be a herdsman's hut. The dwelling in the middle of the vale was a very pleasing object. I said within myself, How quietly might a family live in this pensive solitude, cultivating and loving their own fields! but the herdsman's hut, being the only one in the vale, had a melancholy face; not being attached to any particular plot of land, one could not help considering it as just kept alive and above ground by some dreary connexion with the long barren tract we had travelled through.

The afternoon had been exceedingly pleasant after we had left the vale of Arrochar; the sky was often threatening, but the rain blew off, and the evening was uncommonly fine. The sun had set a short time before we had dismounted from the car to walk up the steep hill at the end of the glen.

Clouds were moving all over the sky—some of a brilliant yellow hue, which shed a light like bright moonlight upon the mountains. We could not have seen the head of the valley under more favourable circumstances.

The passing away of a storm is always a time of life and cheerfulness, especially in a mountainous country; but that afternoon and evening the sky was in an extraordinary degree vivid and beautiful. We often stopped in ascending the hill to look down the long reach of the glen. The road, following the course of the river as far as we could see, the farm and cottage hills, smooth towards the base and rocky higher up, were the sole objects before us. This part of Glen Croe reminded us of some of the dales of the north of England—Grisdale above Ulswater, for instance; but the length of it, and the broad highway, which is always to be seen at a great distance, a sort of centre of the vale, a point of reference, gives to the whole of the glen, and each division of it, a very different character.

At the top of the hill we came to a seat with the well-known inscription, 'Rest and be thankful.' On the same stone it was recorded that the road had been made by Col. Wade's regiment. The seat is placed so as to command a full view of the valley, and the long, long road, which, with the fact recorded, and the exhortation, makes it an affecting resting-place. We called to mind with pleasure a seat under the braes of Loch Lomond on which I had rested, where the traveller is informed by an inscription upon a stone that the road was made by Col. Lascelles' regiment. There, the spot had not been chosen merely as a resting-place, for there was no steep ascent in the highway, but it might be for the sake of a spring of water and a beautiful rock, or, more probably, because at that point the labour had been more than usually toilsome in hewing through the rock. Soon after we had climbed the hill we began to descend into another glen, called Glen Kinglas. We now saw the western sky, which had hitherto been hidden from us by the hill—a glorious mass of clouds uprising from a sea of distant mountains, stretched out in length before us, towards the west—and close by us was a small lake or tarn. From the reflection of the crimson clouds the water appeared of a deep red, like melted rubies, yet with a mixture of a grey or blackish hue: the gorgeous light of the sky, with the singular colour of the lake, made the scene exceedingly romantic; yet it was more melancholy than cheerful. With all the power of light from the clouds, there was an overcasting of the gloom of evening, a twilight upon the hills.

We descended rapidly into the glen, which resembles the lower part of Glen Croe, though it seemed to be inferior in beauty; but before we had passed through one reach it was quite dark, and I only know that the steeps were high, and that we had the company of a foaming stream; and many a vagrant torrent crossed us, dashing down the hills. The road was bad, and, uncertain how we should fare, we were eager and somewhat uneasy to get forward; but when we were out of the close glen, and near to Cairndow, as a traveller had told us, the moon showed her clear face in the sky, revealing a spacious vale, with a broad loch and sloping corn fields; the hills not very high. This cheerful sight put us into spirits, and we thought it was at least no dismal place to sit up all night in, if they had no beds, and they could not refuse us a shelter. We were, however, well received, and sate down in a neat parlour with a good fire.

Tuesday, August 30th.—Breakfasted before our departure, and ate a herring, fresh from the water, at our landlord's earnest recommendation—much superior to the herrings we get in the north of England. Though we rose at seven, could not set off before nine o'clock; the servants were in bed; the kettle did not boil—indeed, we were completely out of patience; but it had always been so, and we resolved to go off in future without breakfast. Cairndow is a single house by the side of the loch, I believe resorted to by gentlemen in the fishing season: it is a pleasant place for such a purpose; but the vale did not look so beautiful as by moonlight—it had a sort of sea-coldness without mountain grandeur. There is a ferry for foot-passengers from Cairndow to the other side of the water, and the road along which all carriages go is carried round the head of the lake, perhaps a distance of three miles.

After we had passed the landing-place of the ferry opposite to Cairndow we saw the lake spread out to a great width, more like an arm of the sea or a great river than one of our lakes; it reminded us of the Severn at the Chepstow passage; but the shores were less rich and the hills higher. The sun shone, which made the morning cheerful, though there was a cold wind. Our road never carried us far from the lake, and with the beating of the waves, the sparkling sunshiny water, boats, the opposite hills, and, on the side on which we travelled, the chance cottages, the coppice woods, and common business of the fields, the ride could not but be amusing. But what most excited our attention was, at one particular place, a cluster of fishing-boats at anchor in a still corner of the lake, a small bay or harbour by the wayside. They were overshadowed by fishermen's nets hung out to dry, which formed a dark awning that covered them like a tent, overhanging the water on each side, and falling in the most exquisitely graceful folds.

There was a monastic pensiveness, a funereal gloom in the appearance of this little company of vessels, which was the more interesting from the general liveliness and glancing motions of the water, they being perfectly still and silent in their sheltered nook.

When we had travelled about seven miles from Cairndow, winding round the bottom of a hill, we came in view of a great basin or elbow of the lake. Completely out of sight of the long track of water we had coasted, we seemed now to be on the edge of a very large, almost circular, lake, the town of Inverary before us, a line of white buildings on a low promontory right opposite, and close to the water's edge; the whole landscape a showy scene, and bursting upon us at once. A traveller who was riding by our side called out, 'Can that be the Castle?' Recollecting the prints which we had seen, we knew it could not; but the mistake is a natural one at that distance: it is so little like an ordinary town, from the mixture of regularity and irregularity in the buildings. With the expanse of water and pleasant mountains, the scattered boats and sloops, and those gathered together, it had a truly festive appearance. A few steps more brought us in view of the Castle, a stately turreted mansion, but with a modern air, standing on a lawn, retired from the water, and screened behind by woods covering the sides of high hills to the top, and still beyond, by bare mountains. Our road wound round the semicircular shore, crossing two bridges of lordly architecture. The town looked pretty when we drew near to it in connexion with its situation, different from any place I had ever seen, yet exceedingly like what I imaged to myself from representations in raree-shows, or pictures of foreign places—Venice, for example—painted on the scene of a play-house, which one is apt to fancy are as cleanly and gay as they look through the magnifying-glass of the raree-show or in the candle-light dazzle of a theatre. At the door of the inn, though certainly the buildings had not that delightful outside which they appeared to have at a distance, yet they looked very pleasant. The range bordering on the water consisted of little else than the inn, being a large house, with very large stables, the county gaol, the opening into the main street into the town, and an arched gateway, the entrance into the Duke of Argyle's private domain.

We were decently well received at the inn, but it was over-rich in waiters and large rooms to be exactly to our taste, though quite in harmony with the neighbourhood. Before dinner we went into the Duke's pleasure-grounds, which are extensive, and of course command a variety of lively and interesting views. Walked through avenues of tall beech-trees, and observed some that we thought even the tallest we had ever seen; but they were all scantily covered with leaves, and the leaves exceedingly small—indeed, some of them, in the most exposed situations, were almost bare, as if it had been winter. Travellers who wish to view the inside of the Castle send in their names, and the Duke appoints the time of their going; but we did not think that what we should see would repay us for the trouble, there being no pictures, and the house, which I believe has not been built above half a century, is fitted up in the modern style. If there had been any reliques of the ancient costume of the castle of a High-land chieftain, we should have been sorry to have passed it.

Sate after dinner by the fireside till near sunset, for it was very cold, though the sun shone all day. At the beginning of this our second walk we passed through the town, which is but a doleful example of Scotch filth. The houses are plastered or rough-cast, and washed yellow—well built, well sized, and sash-windowed, bespeaking a connexion with the Duke, such a dependence as may be expected in a small town so near to his mansion; and indeed he seems to have done his utmost to make them comfortable, according to our English notions of comfort: they are fit for the houses of people living decently upon a decent trade; but the windows and door-steads were as dirty as in a dirty by-street of a large town, making a most unpleasant contrast with the comely face of the buildings towards the water, and the ducal grandeur and natural festivity of the scene. Smoke and blackness are the wild growth of a Highland hut: the mud floors cannot be washed, the door-steads are trampled by cattle, and if the inhabitants be not very cleanly it gives one little pain; but dirty people living in two-storied stone houses, with dirty sash windows, are a melancholy spectacle anywhere, giving the notion either of vice or the extreme of wretchedness.

Returning through the town, we went towards the Castle, and entered the Duke's grounds by a porter's lodge, following the carriage-road through the park, which is prettily scattered over with trees, and slopes gently towards the lake. A great number of lime-trees were growing singly, not beautiful in their shape, but I mention them for the resemblance to one of the same kind we had seen in the morning, which formed a shade as impenetrable as the roof of any house. The branches did not spread far, nor any one branch much further than another; on the outside it was like a green bush shorn with shears, but when we sate upon a bench under it, looking upwards, in the middle of the tree we could not perceive any green at all; it was like a hundred thousand magpies' nests clustered and matted together, the twigs and boughs being so intertwined that neither the light of the mid-day sun nor showers of hail or rain could pierce through them. The lime-trees on the lawn resembled this tree both in shape and in the manner of intertwisting their twigs, but they were much smaller, and not an impenetrable shade.

The views from the Castle are delightful. Opposite is the lake, girt with mountains, or rather smooth high hills; to the left appears a very steep rocky hill, called Duniquoich Hill, on the top of which is a building like a watch-tower; it rises boldly and almost perpendicular from the plain, at a little distance from the river Arey, that runs through the grounds. To the right is the town, overtopped by a sort of spire or pinnacle of the church, a thing unusual in Scotland, except in the large towns, and which would often give an elegant appearance to the villages, which, from the uniformity of the huts, and the frequent want of tall trees, they seldom exhibit.

In looking at an extensive prospect, or travelling through a large vale, the Trough of the Clyde for instance, I could not help thinking that in England there would have been somewhere a tower or spire to warn us of a village lurking under the covert of a wood or bank, or to point out some particular spot on the distant hills which we might look at with kindly feelings. I well remember how we used to love the little nest of trees out of which Ganton spire rose on the distant Wolds opposite to the windows at Gallow Hill. The spire of Inverary is not of so beautiful a shape as those of the English churches, and, not being one of a class of buildings which is understood at once, seen near or at a distance, is a less interesting object; but it suits well with the outlandish trimness of the buildings bordering on the water; indeed, there is no one thing of the many gathered together in the extensive circuit of the basin or vale of Inverary, that is not in harmony with the effect of the whole place. The Castle is built of a beautiful hewn stone, in colour resembling our blue slates. The author-tourists have quarrelled with the architecture of it, but we did not find much that we were disposed to blame. A castle in a deep glen, overlooking a roaring stream, and defended by precipitous rocks, is, no doubt, an object far more interesting; but, dropping all ideas of danger or insecurity, the natural retinue in our minds of an ancient Highland chieftain,—take a Duke of Argyle at the end of the eighteenth century, let him have his house in Grosvenor Square, his London liveries, and daughters glittering at St. James's, and I think you will be satisfied with his present mansion in the Highlands, which seems to suit with the present times and its situation, and that is indeed a noble one for a modern Duke of the mountainous district of Argyleshire, with its bare valleys, its rocky coasts, and sea lochs.

There is in the natural endowments of Inverary something akin to every feature of the general character of the county; yet even the very mountains and the lake itself have a kind of princely festivity in their appearance. I do not know how to communicate the feeling, but it seemed as if it were no insult to the hills to look on them as the shield and enclosure of the ducal domain, to which the water might delight in bearing its tribute. The hills near the lake are smooth, so smooth that they might have been shaven or swept; the shores, too, had somewhat of the same effect, being bare, and having no roughness, no woody points; yet the whole circuit being very large, and the hills so extensive, the scene was not the less cheerful and festive, rejoicing in the light of heaven. Behind the Castle the hills are planted to a great height, and the pleasure-grounds extend far up the valley of Arey. We continued our walk a short way along the river, and were sorry to see it stripped of its natural ornaments, after the fashion of Mr. Brown, and left to tell its tale—for it would not be silent like the river at Blenheim—to naked fields and the planted trees on the hills. We were disgusted with the stables, outhouses, or farm-houses in different parts of the grounds behind the Castle: they were broad, out-spreading, fantastic, and unintelligible buildings.

Sate in the park till the moonlight was perceived more than the light of day. We then walked near the town by the water-side. I observed that the children who were playing did not speak Erse, but a much worse English than is spoken by those Highlanders whose common language is the Erse. I went into the town to purchase tea and sugar to carry with us on our journey. We were tired when we returned to the inn, and went to bed directly after tea. My room was at the very top of the house—one flight of steps after another!—but when I drew back the curtains of my window I was repaid for the trouble of panting up-stairs by one of the most splendid moonlight prospects that can be conceived: the whole circuit of the hills, the Castle, the two bridges, the tower on Duniquoich Hill, and the lake with many boats—fit scene for summer midnight festivities! I should have liked to have seen a bevy of Scottish ladies sailing, with music, in a gay barge. William, to whom I have read this, tells me that I have used the very words of Browne of Ottery, Coleridge's fellow-townsman:—

> 'As I have seen when on the breast of Thames
> A heavenly bevy of sweet English dames,
> In some calm evening of delightful May,
> With music give a farewell to the day,
> Or as they would (with an admired tone)
> Greet night's ascension to her ebon throne.'

BROWNE's Britannia's Pastorals.

Wednesday, August 31st. —We had a long day's journey before us, without a regular baiting-place on the road, so we breakfasted at Inverary, and did not set off till nine o'clock, having, as usual, to complain of the laziness of the servants.

Our road was up the valley behind the Castle, the same we had gone along the evening before. Further up, though the plantations on the hills are noble, the valley was cold and naked, wanting hedgerows and comfortable houses. We travelled several miles under the plantations, the vale all along seeming to belong almost exclusively to the Castle. It might have been better distinguished and adorned, as we thought, by neater farm-houses and cottages than are common in Scotland, and snugger fields with warm hedgerows, at the same time testifying as boldly its adherence to the chief.

At that point of the valley where the pleasure-grounds appear to end, we left our horse at a cottage door, and turned a few steps out of the road to see a waterfall, which roared so loud that we could not have gone by without looking about for it, even if we had not known that there was one near Inverary. The waterfall is not remarkable for anything but the good taste with which it has been left to itself, though there is a pleasure-road from the Castle to it. As we went further up the valley the roads died away, and it became an ordinary Scotch glen, the poor pasturage of the hills creeping down into the valley, where it was little better for the shelter, I mean little greener than on the hill-sides; but a man must be of a churlish nature if, with a mind free to look about, he should not find such a glen a pleasing place to travel through, though seeing little but the busy brook, with here and there a bush or tree, and cattle pasturing near the thinly-scattered dwellings. But we came to one spot which I cannot forget, a single green field at the junction of another brook with the Arey, a peninsula surrounded with a close row of trees, which overhung the streams, and under their branches we could just see a neat white house that stood in the middle of the field enclosed by the trees. Before us was nothing but bare hills, and the road through the bare glen. A person who has not travelled in Scotland can scarcely imagine the pleasure we have had from a stone house, though fresh from the workmen's hands, square and sharp; there is generally such an appearance of equality in poverty through the long glens of Scotland, giving the notion of savage ignorance—no house better than another, and barns and houses all alike. This house had, however, other recommendations of its own; even in the fertile parts of Somersetshire it would have been a delicious spot; here, 'Mid mountain wild set like a little nest,' it was a resting-place for the fancy, and to this day I often think of it, the cottage and its green covert, as an image of romance, a place of which I have the same sort of knowledge as of some of the retirements, the little valleys, described so livelily by Spenser in his Fairy Queen.

We travelled on, the glen now becoming entirely bare. Passed a miserable hut on a naked hill-side, not far from the road, where we were told by a man who came out of it that we might refresh ourselves with a dram of whisky. Went over the hill, and saw nothing remarkable till we came in view of Loch Awe, a large lake far below us, among high mountains—one very large mountain right opposite, which we afterwards found was called Cruachan. The day was pleasant—sunny gleams and a fresh breeze; the lake— we looked across it—as bright as silver, which made the islands, three or four in number, appear very green. We descended gladly, invited by the prospect before us, travelling downwards, along the side of the hill, above a deep glen, woody towards the lower part near the brook; the hills on all sides were high and bare, and not very stony: it made us think of the descent from Newlands into Buttermere, though on a wider scale, and much inferior in simple majesty.

After walking down the hill a long way we came to a bridge, under which the water dashed through a dark channel of rocks among trees, the lake being at a considerable distance below, with cultivated lands between. Close upon the bridge was a small hamlet, a few houses near together, and huddled up in trees—a very sweet spot, the only retired village we had yet seen which was characterized by 'beautiful' wildness with sheltering warmth. We had been told at Inverary that we should come to a place where we might give our horse a feed of corn, and found on inquiry that there was a little public-house here, or rather a hut 'where they kept a dram.' It was a cottage, like all the rest, without a sign-board. The woman of the house helped to take the horse out of harness, and, being hungry, we asked her if she could make us some porridge, to which she replied that 'we should get that,' and I followed her into the house, and sate over her hearth while she was making it. As to fire, there was little sign of it, save the smoke, for a long time, she having no fuel but green wood, and no bellows but her breath. My eyes smarted exceedingly, but the woman seemed so kind and cheerful that I was willing to endure it for the sake of warming my feet in the ashes and talking to her. The fire was in the middle of the room, a crook being suspended from a cross-beam, and a hole left at the top for the smoke to find its way out by: it was a rude Highland hut, unadulterated by Lowland fashions, but it had not the elegant shape of the ferry-house at Loch Ketterine, and the fire, being in the middle of the room, could not be such a snug place to draw to on a winter's night.

We had a long afternoon before us, with only eight miles to travel to Dalmally, and, having been told that a ferry-boat was kept at one of the islands, we resolved to call for it, and row to the island, so we went to the top of an eminence, and the man who was with us set some children to work to gather sticks and withered leaves to make a smoky fire—a signal for the boatman, whose hut is on a flat green island, like a sheep pasture, without trees, and of a considerable size: the man told us it was a rabbit-warren. There were other small islands, on one of which was a ruined house, fortification, or small castle: we could not learn anything of its history, only a girl told us that formerly gentlemen lived in such places. Immediately from the water's edge rose the mountain Cruachan on the opposite side of the lake; it is woody near the water and craggy above, with deep hollows on the surface. We thought it the grandest mountain we had seen, and on saying to the man who was with us that it was a fine mountain, 'Yes,' he replied, 'it is an excellent mountain,' adding that it was higher than Ben Lomond, and then told us some wild stories of the enormous profits it brought to Lord Breadalbane, its lawful owner. The shape of Loch Awe is very remarkable, its outlet being at one side, and only about eight miles from the head, and the whole lake twenty-four miles in length. We looked with longing after that branch of it opposite to us out of which the water issues: it seemed almost like a river gliding under steep precipices. What we saw of the larger branch, or what might be called the body of the lake, was less promising, the banks being merely gentle slopes, with not very high mountains behind, and the ground moorish and cold.

The children, after having collected fuel for our fire, began to play on the green hill where we stood, as heedless as if we had been trees or stones, and amused us exceedingly with their activity: they wrestled, rolled down the hill, pushing one another over and over again, laughing, screaming, and chattering Erse: they were all without shoes and stockings, which, making them fearless of hurting or being hurt, gave a freedom to the action of their limbs which I never saw in English children: they stood upon one another, body, breast, or face, or any other part; sometimes one was uppermost, sometimes another, and sometimes they rolled all together, so that we could not know to which body this leg or that arm belonged. We waited, watching them, till we were assured that the boatman had noticed our signal—By the bye, if we had received proper directions at Loch Lomond, on our journey to Loch Ketterine, we should have made our way down the lake till we had come opposite to the ferryman's house, where there is a hut, and the people who live there are accustomed to call him by the same signal as here. Luckily for us we were not so well instructed, for we should have missed the pleasure of receiving the kindness of Mr. and Mrs. Macfarlane and their family.

A young woman who wanted to go to the island accompanied us to the water-side. The walk was pleasant, through fields with hedgerows, the greenest fields we had seen in Scotland; but we were obliged to return without going to the island. The poor man had taken his boat to another place, and the waters were swollen so that we could not go close to the shore, and show ourselves to him, nor could we make him hear by shouting. On our return to the public-house we asked the woman what we should pay her, and were not a little surprised when she answered, 'Three shillings.' Our horse had had a sixpenny feed of miserable corn, not worth threepence; the rest of the charge was for skimmed milk, oat-bread, porridge, and blue milk cheese: we told her it was far too much; and, giving her half-a-crown, departed. I was sorry she had made this unreasonable demand, because we had liked the woman, and we had before been so well treated in the Highland cottages; but, on thinking more about it, I satisfied myself that it was no scheme to impose upon us, for she was contented with the half-crown, and would, I daresay, have been so with two shillings, if we had offered it her at first. Not being accustomed to fix a price upon porridge and milk, to such as we, at least, when we asked her she did not know what to say; but, seeing that we were travelling for pleasure, no doubt she concluded we were rich, and that what was a small gain to her could be no great loss to us.

When we had gone a little way we saw before us a young man with a bundle over his shoulder, hung on a stick, bearing a great boy on his back: seeing that they were travellers, we offered to take the boy on the car, to which the man replied that he should be more than thankful, and set him up beside me. They had walked from Glasgow, and that morning from Inverary; the boy was only six years old, 'But,' said his father, 'he is a stout walker,' and a fine fellow he was, smartly dressed in tight clean clothes and a nice round hat: he was going to stay with his grandmother at Dalmally. I found him good company; though I could not draw a single word out of him, it was a pleasure to see his happiness gleaming through the shy glances of his healthy countenance. Passed a pretty chapel by the lake-side, and an island with a farm-house upon it, and corn and pasture fields; but, as we went along, we had frequent reason to regret the want of English hedgerows and English culture; for the ground was often swampy or moorish near the lake where comfortable dwellings among green fields might have been. When we came near to the end of the lake we had a steep hill to climb, so William and I walked; and we had such confidence in our horse that we were not afraid to leave the car to his guidance with the child in it; we were soon, however, alarmed at seeing him trot up the hill a long way before us; the child, having raised himself up upon the seat, was beating him as hard as he could with a little stick which he carried in his hand; and when he saw our eyes were on him he sate down, I believe very sorry to resign his office: the horse slackened his pace, and no accident happened.

When we had ascended half-way up the hill, directed by the man, I took a nearer footpath, and at the top came in view of a most impressive scene, a ruined castle on an island almost in the middle of the last compartment of the lake, backed by a mountain cove, down which came a roaring stream. The castle occupied every foot of the island that was visible to us, appearing to rise out of the water; mists rested upon the mountain side, with spots of sunshine between; there was a mild desolation in the low grounds, a solemn grandeur in the mountains, and the castle was wild, yet stately, not dismantled of its turrets, nor the walls broken down, though completely in ruin. After having stood some minutes I joined William on the high road, and both wishing to stay longer near this place, we requested the man to drive his little boy on to Dalmally, about two miles further, and leave the car at the inn. He told us that the ruin was called Kilchurn Castle, that it belonged to Lord Breadalbane, and had been built by one of the ladies of that family for her defence during her Lord's absence at the Crusades, for which purpose she levied a tax of seven years' rent upon her tenants; he said that from that side of the lake it did not appear, in very dry weather, to stand upon an island; but that it was possible to go over to it without being wet-shod. We were very lucky in seeing it after a great flood; for its enchanting effect was chiefly owing to its situation in the lake, a decayed palace rising out of the plain of waters! I have called it a palace, for such feeling it gave to me, though having been built as a place of defence, a castle or fortress. We turned again and reascended the hill, and sate a long time in the middle of it looking on the castle and the huge mountain cove opposite,

and William, addressing himself to the ruin, poured out
these verses:—

> Child of loud-throated War! the mountain stream
> Roars in thy hearing; but thy hour of rest
> Is come, and thou art silent in thy age.

We walked up the hill again, and, looking down the vale,
had a fine view of the lake and islands, resembling the views
down Windermere, though much less rich. Our walk to
Dalmally was pleasant: the vale makes a turn to the right,
beyond the head of the lake, and the village of Dalmally,
which is, in fact, only a few huts, the manse or minister's
house, the chapel, and the inn, stands near the river, which
flows into the head of the lake. The whole vale is very
pleasing, the lower part of the hill-sides being sprinkled with
thatched cottages, cultivated ground in small patches near
them, which evidently belonged to the cottages.

We were overtaken by a gentleman who rode on a
beautiful white pony, like Lilly, and was followed by his
servant, a Highland boy, on another pony, a little creature,
not much bigger than a large mastiff, on which were slung a
pair of crutches and a tartan plaid. The gentleman entered
into conversation with us, and on our telling him that
we were going to Glen Coe, he advised us, instead of
proceeding directly to Tyndrum, the next stage, to go round
by the outlet of Loch Awe to Loch Etive, and thence to
Glen Coe. We were glad to change our plan, for we wanted
much to see more of Loch Awe, and he told us that the
whole of the way by Loch Etive was pleasant, and the road
to Tyndrum as dreary as possible; indeed, we could see it at
that time several miles before us upon the side of a bleak
mountain; and he said that there was nothing but moors
and mountains all the way. We reached the inn a little
before sunset, ordered supper, and I walked out. Crossed a

bridge to look more nearly at the parsonage-house and the chapel, which stands upon a bank close to the river, a pretty stream overhung in some parts by trees. The vale is very pleasing; but, like all the other Scotch vales we had yet seen, it told of its kinship with the mountains and of poverty or some neglect on the part of man.

Thursday, September 1st. — We had been attended at supper by a civil boy, whom we engaged to rouse us at six o'clock, and to provide us each a basin of milk and bread, and have the car ready; all which he did punctually, and we were off in good time. The morning was not unpleasant, though rather cold, and we had some fear of rain. Crossed the bridge, and passed by the manse and chapel, our road carrying us back again in the direction we had come; but on the opposite side of the river. Passed close to many of the houses we had seen on the hill-side, which the lame gentleman had told us belonged to Lord Breadalbane, and were attached to little farms, or 'crofts,' as he called them. Lord Breadalbane had lately laid out a part of his estates in this way as an experiment, in the hope of preventing discontent and emigration. We were sorry we had not an opportunity of seeing into these cottages, and of learning how far the people were happy or otherwise. The dwellings certainly did not look so comfortable when we were near to them as from a distance; but this might be chiefly owing to what the inhabitants did not feel as an evil—the dirt about the doors. We saw, however—a sight always painful to me—two or three women, each creeping after her single cow, while it was feeding on the slips of grass between the corn-grounds. Went round the head of the lake, and onwards close to the lake-side. Kilchurn Castle was always interesting, though not so grand as seen from the other side, with its own mountain cove and roaring stream. It combined with the vale of Dalmally and the distant hills—a beautiful scene, yet overspread with a gentle desolation. As we went further down we lost sight of the vale of Dalmally. The castle, which we often stopped to look back upon, was very beautiful seen in combination with the opposite shore of the lake—perhaps a little bay, a tuft of trees, or a slope of the hill. Travelled under the foot of the mountain Cruachan, along an excellent road, having the lake close to us on our left, woods overhead, and frequent torrents tumbling down the hills. The distant views across the lake were not peculiarly interesting after we were out of sight of Kilchurn Castle, the lake being wide, and the opposite shore not rich, and those mountains which we could see were not high.

Came opposite to the village where we had dined the day before, and, losing sight of the body of the lake, pursued the narrow channel or pass, which is, I believe, three miles long, out of which issues the river that flows into Loch Etive. We were now enclosed between steep hills, on the opposite side entirely bare, on our side bare or woody; the branch of the lake generally filling the whole area of the vale. It was a pleasing, solitary scene; the long reach of naked precipices on the other side rose directly out of the water, exceedingly steep, not rugged or rocky, but with scanty sheep pasturage and large beds of small stones, purple, dove-coloured, or red, such as are called Screes in Cumberland and Westmoreland. These beds, or rather streams of stones, appeared as smooth as the turf itself, nay, I might say, as soft as the feathers of birds, which they resembled in colour. There was no building on either side of the water; in many parts only just room for the road, and on the other shore no footing, as it might seem, for any creature larger than the mountain sheep, and they, in treading amongst the shelving stones, must often send them down into the lake below.

After we had wound for some time through the valley, having met neither foot-traveller, horse, nor cart, we started at the sight of a single vessel, just as it turned round the point of a hill, coming into the reach of the valley where we were. She floated steadily through the middle of the water, with one large sail spread out, full swollen by the breeze, that blew her right towards us. I cannot express what romantic images this vessel brought along with her—how much more beautiful the mountains appeared, the lake how much more graceful. There was one man on board, who sate at the helm, and he, having no companion, made the boat look more silent than if we could not have seen him. I had almost said the ship, for on that narrow water it appeared as large as the ships which I have watched sailing out of a harbour of the sea. A little further on we passed a stone hut by the lake-side, near which were many charcoal sacks, and we conjectured that the vessel had been depositing charcoal brought from other parts of Loch Awe to be carried to the iron-works at Loch Ètive. A little further on we came to the end of the lake, but where exactly it ended was not easy to determine, for the river was as broad as the lake, and we could only say when it became positively a river by the rushing of the water. It is, indeed, a grand stream, the quantity of water being very large, frequently forming rapids, and always flowing very quickly; but its greatness is short-lived, for, after a course of three miles, it is lost in the great waters of Loch Etive, a sea loch.

Crossed a bridge, and climbing a hill towards Taynuilt, our baiting-place, we saw a hollow to the right below us, through which the river continued its course between rocks and steep banks of wood. William turned aside to look into the dell, but I was too much tired. We had left it, two or three hundred yards behind, an open river, the hills, enclosing the branch of the lake, having settled down into irregular slopes. We were glad when we reached Taynuilt, a village of huts, with a chapel and one stone house, which was the inn. It had begun to rain, and I was almost benumbed with the cold, besides having a bad headache; so it rejoiced me to see kind looks on the landlady's face, and that she was willing to put herself in a bustle for our comfort; we had a good fire presently, and breakfast was set out—eggs, preserved gooseberries, excellent cream, cheese, and butter, but no wheat bread, and the oaten cakes were so hard I could not chew them. We wished to go upon Loch Etive; so, having desired the landlady to prepare a fowl for supper, and engaged beds, which she promised us willingly—a proof that we were not in the great road—we determined to find our way to the lake and endeavour to procure a boat. It rained heavily, but we went on, hoping the sky would clear up.

Walked through unenclosed fields, a sort of half-desolate country; but when we came to the mouth of the river which issues out of Loch Awe, and which we had to cross by a ferry, looking up that river we saw that the vale down which it flowed was richly wooded and beautiful.

We were now among familiar fireside names. We could see the town of Bunawe, a place of which the old woman with whom William lodged ten years at Hawkshead used to tell tales half as long as an ancient romance. It is a small village or port on the same side of Loch Etive on which we stood, and at a little distance is a house built by a Mr. Knott of Coniston Water-head, a partner in the iron-foundry at Bunawe, in the service of whose family the old woman had spent her youth. It was an ugly yellow-daubed building, staring this way and that, but William looked at it with pleasure for poor Ann Tyson's sake. We hailed the ferry-boat, and a little boy came to fetch us; he rowed up against the stream with all his might for a considerable way, and then yielding to it, the boat was shot towards the shore almost like an arrow from a bow. It was pleasing to observe the dexterity with which the lad managed his oars, glorying in the appearance of danger—for he observed us watching him, and afterwards, while he conveyed us over, his pride redoubled; for my part, I was completely dizzy with the swiftness of the motion.

We could not have a boat from the ferry, but were told that if we would walk to a house half a mile up the river, we had a chance of getting one. I went a part of the way with William, and then sate down under the umbrella near some houses. A woman came out to talk with me, and pressed me to take shelter in her house, which I refused, afraid of missing William. She eyed me with extreme curiosity, asking fifty questions respecting the object of our journey. She told me that it rained most parts of the year there, and that there was no chance of fine weather that day; and I believe when William came to tell me that we could have a boat, she thought I was half crazed. We went down to the shore of the lake, and, after having sate some time under a wall, the boatman came to us, and we went upon the water. At first it did not rain heavily, and the air was not cold, and before we had gone far we rejoiced that we had not been faint-hearted. The loch is of a considerable width, but the mountains are so very high that, whether we were close under them or looked from one shore to the other, they maintained their dignity. I speak of the higher part of the loch, above the town of Bunawe and the large river, for downwards they are but hills, and the water spreads out wide towards undetermined shores. On our right was the mountain Cruachan, rising directly from the lake, and on the opposite side another mountain, called Ben Durinish, craggy, and exceedingly steep, with wild wood growing among the rocks and stones.

We crossed the water, which was very rough in the middle, but calmer near the shores, and some of the rocky basins and little creeks among the rocks were as still as a mirror, and they were so beautiful with the reflection of the orange-coloured seaweed growing on the stones or rocks, that a child, with a child's delight in gay colours, might have danced with joy at the sight of them. It never ceased raining, and the tops of the mountains were concealed by mists, but as long as we could see across the water we were contented; for though little could be seen of the true shapes and permanent appearances of the mountains, we saw enough to give us the most exquisite delight: the powerful lake which filled the large vale, roaring torrents, clouds floating on the mountain sides, sheep that pastured there, sea-birds and land birds. We sailed a considerable way without coming to any houses or cultivated fields. There was no horse-road on either side of the loch, but a person on foot, as the boatman told us, might make his way at the foot of Ben Durinish, namely on that side of the loch on which we were; there was, however, not the least track to be seen, and it must be very difficult and laborious.

We happened to say that we were going to Glen Coe, which would be the journey of a long day and a half, when one of the men, pointing to the head of the loch, replied that if we were there we should be but an hour's walk from Glen Coe. Though it continued raining, and there was no hope that the rain would cease, we could not help wishing to go by that way: it was an adventure; we were not afraid of trusting ourselves to the hospitality of the Highlanders, and we wanted to give our horse a day's rest, his back having been galled by the saddle. The owner of the boat, who understood English much better than the other man, his helper, said he would make inquiries about the road at a farm-house a little further on. He was very ready to talk with us, and was rather an interesting companion; he spoke after a slow and solemn manner, in book and sermon language and phrases:

> "A stately speech, such as grave livers do in Scotland use."

When we came to the farm-house of which the man had spoken, William and he landed to make the necessary inquiries. It was a thatched house at the foot of the high mountain Ben Durinish—a few patches or little beds of corn belonging to it; but the spot was pastoral, the green grass growing to the walls of the house. The dwelling-house was distinguished from the outer buildings, which were numerous, making it look like two or three houses, as is common in Scotland, by a chimney and one small window with sash-panes; on one side was a little woody glen, with a precipitous stream that fell into the bay, which was perfectly still, and bordered with the rich orange-colour reflected from the sea-weed. Cruachan, on the other side of the lake, was exceedingly grand, and appeared of an enormous height, spreading out two large arms that made a cove down which fell many streams swoln by the rain, and in the hollow of the cove were some huts which looked like a village. The top of the mountain was concealed from us by clouds, and the mists floated high and low upon the sides of it.

William came back to the boat highly pleased with the cheerful hospitality and kindness of the woman of the house, who would scarcely permit him and his guide to go away without taking some refreshment. She was the only person at home, so they could not obtain the desired information; but William had been well repaid for the trouble of landing; indeed, rainy as it was, I regretted that I had not landed also, for I should have wished to bear away in my memory a perfect image of this place,—the view from the doors, as well as the simple Highland comforts and contrivances which were near it. I think I never saw a retirement that would have so completely satisfied me, if I had wanted to be altogether shut out from the world, and at the same time among the grandest of the works of God; but it must be remembered that mountains are often so much dignified by clouds, mists, and other accidents of weather, that one could not know them again in the full sunshine of a summer's noon. But, whatever the mountains may be in their own shapes, the farm-house with its pastoral grounds and corn fields won from the mountain, its warm out-houses in irregular stages one above another on the side of the hill, the rocks, the stream, and sheltering bay, must at all times be interesting objects. The household boat lay at anchor, chained to a rock, which, like the whole border of the lake, was edged with sea-weed, and some fishing-nets were hung upon poles,—affecting images, which led our thoughts out to the wide ocean, yet made these solitudes of the mountains bear the impression of greater safety and more deep seclusion.

The rain became so heavy that we should certainly have turned back if we had not felt more than usual courage from the pleasure we had enjoyed, which raised hope where none was. There were some houses a little higher up, and we determined to go thither and make further inquiries. We could now hardly see to the other side of the lake, yet continued to go on, and presently heard some people pushing through a thicket close to us, on which the boatman called out, 'There's one that can tell us something about the road to Glen Coe, for he was born there.' We looked up and saw a ragged, lame fellow, followed by some others, with a fishing-rod over his shoulder; and he was making such good speed through the boughs that one might have half believed he was the better for his lame leg. He was the head of a company of tinkers, who, as the men told us, travel with their fishing-rods as duly as their hammers. On being hailed by us the whole company stopped; and their lame leader and our boatmen shouted to each other in Erse—a savage cry to our ears, in that lonely and romantic place. We could not learn from the tinker all we wished to know, therefore when we came near to the houses William landed again with the owner of the boat. The rain was now so heavy that we could see nothing at all—not even the houses whither William was going.

We had given up all thought of proceeding further at that time, but were desirous to know how far that road to Glen Coe was practicable for us. They met with an intelligent man, who was at work with others in a hay field, though it rained so heavily; he gave them the information they desired, and said that there was an acquaintance of his between that place and Glen Coe, who, he had no doubt, would gladly accommodate us with lodging and anything else we might need. When William returned to the boat we shaped our course back again down the water, leaving the head of Loch Etive not only unvisited, but unseen—to our great regret. The rain was very heavy; the wind had risen, and both wind and tide were against us, so that it was hard labour for the boatmen to push us on. They kept as close to the shore as they could, to be under the wind; but at the doubling of many of the rocky points the tide was so strong that it was difficult to get on at all, and I was sometimes afraid that we should be dashed against the rocks, though I believe, indeed, there was not much danger.

Came down the same side of the lake under Ben Durinish, and landed at a ferry-house opposite to Bunawe, where we gave the men a glass of whisky; but our chief motive for landing was to look about the place, which had a most wild aspect at that time. It was a low promontory, pushed far into the water, narrowing the lake exceedingly; in the obscurity occasioned by the mist and rain it appeared to be an island; it was stained and weather-beaten, a rocky place, seeming to bear no produce but such as might be cherished by cold and storms, lichens or the incrustations of sea rocks. We rowed right across the water to the mouth of the river of Loch Awe, our boat following the ferry-boat which was conveying the tinker crew to the other side, whither they were going to lodge, as the men told us, in some kiln, which they considered as their right and privilege—a lodging always to be found where there was any arable land—for every farm has its kiln to dry the corn in: another proof of the wetness of the climate. The kilns are built of stone, covered in, and probably as good a shelter as the huts in which these Highland vagrants were born. They gather sticks or heather for their fire, and, as they are obstinate beggars, for the men said they would not be denied, they probably have plenty of food with little other trouble than that of wandering in search of it, for their smutty faces and tinker equipage serve chiefly for a passport to a free and careless life. It rained very heavily, and the wind blew when we crossed the lake, and their boat and ours went tilting over the high waves. They made a romantic appearance; three women were of the party; two men rowed them over; the lame fellow sate at one end of the boat, and his companion at the other, each with an enormous fishing-rod, which looked very graceful, something like masts to the boat. When we had landed at the other side we saw them, after having begged at the ferry-house, strike merrily through the fields, no doubt betaking themselves to their shelter for the night.

We were completely wet when we reached the inn; the landlady wanted to make a fire for me up-stairs, but I went into her own parlour to undress, and her daughter, a pretty little girl, who could speak a few words of English, waited on me; I rewarded her with one of the penny books bought at Dumfries for Johnny, with which she was greatly delighted. We had an excellent supper—fresh salmon, a fowl, gooseberries and cream, and potatoes; good beds; and the next morning boiled milk and bread, and were only charged seven shillings and sixpence for the whole—horse, liquor, supper, and the two breakfasts. We thought they had made a mistake, and told them so—for it was only just half as much as we had paid the day before at Dalmally, the case being that Dalmally is in the main road of the tourists. The landlady insisted on my bringing away a little cup instead of our tin can, which she told me had been taken from the car by some children: we set no little value on this cup as a memorial of the good woman's honesty and kindness, and hoped to have brought it home....

Friday, September 2d. —Departed at about seven o'clock this morning, having to travel eight miles down Loch Etive, and then to cross a ferry. Our road was at first at a considerable distance from the lake, and out of sight of it, among undulating hills covered with coppice woods, resembling the country between Coniston and Windermere, but it afterwards carried us close to the water's edge; and in this part of our ride we were disappointed. We knew that the high mountains were all at the head of the lake, therefore had not expected the same awful grandeur which we beheld the day before, and perceived by glimpses; but the gentleman whom we met with at Dalmally had told us that there were many fine situations for gentlemen's seats on this part of the lake, which had made us expect greater loveliness near the shores, and better cultivation. It is true there are pleasant bays, with grounds prettily sloping to the water, and coppice woods, where houses would stand in shelter and sun, looking on the lake; but much is yet wanting—waste lands to be ploughed, peat-mosses drained, hedgerows reared; and the woods demand a grant of longer life than is now their privilege.

But after we had journeyed about six miles a beautiful scene opened upon us. The morning had been gloomy, and at this time the sun shone out, scattering the clouds. We looked right down the lake, that was covered with streams of dazzling sunshine, which revealed the indentings of the dark shores. On a bold promontory, on the same side of the loch where we were, stood an old castle, an irregular tall building, not without majesty; and beyond, with leagues of water between, our eyes settled upon the island of Mull, a high mountain, green in the sunshine, and overcast with clouds,—an object as inviting to the fancy as the evening sky in the west, and though of a terrestrial green, almost as visionary. We saw that it was an island of the seas but were unacquainted with its name; it was of a gem-like colour, and as soft as the sky. The shores of Loch Etive, in their moorish, rocky wildness, their earthly bareness, as they lay in length before us, produced a contrast which, with the pure sea, the brilliant sunshine, the long distance, contributed to the aërial and romantic power with which the mountain island was invested.

Soon after, we came to the ferry. The boat being on the other shore, we had to wait a considerable time, though the water was not wide, and our call was heard immediately. The boatmen moved with surly tardiness, as if glad to make us know that they were our masters. At this point the lake was narrowed to the breadth of not a very wide river by a round ear or promontory on the side on which we were, and a low ridge of peat-mossy ground on the other. It was a dreary place, shut out from the beautiful prospect of the

Isle of Mull, and Dunstaffnage Castle—so the fortress was called. Four or five men came over with the boat; the horse was unyoked, and being harshly driven over rough stones, which were as slippery as ice, with slimy seaweed, he was in terror before he reached the boat, and they completed the work by beating and pushing him by main force over the ridge of the boat, for there was no open end, or plank, or any other convenience for shipping either horse or carriage. I was very uneasy when we were launched on the water. A blackguard-looking fellow, blind of one eye, which I could not but think had been put out in some strife or other, held him by force like a horse-breaker, while the poor creature fretted, and stamped with his feet against the bare boards, frightening himself more and more with every stroke; and when we were in the middle of the water I would have given a thousand pounds to have been sure that we should reach the other side in safety. The tide was rushing violently in, making a strong eddy with the stream of the loch, so that the motion of the boat and the noise and foam of the waves terrified him still more, and we thought it would be impossible to keep him in the boat, and when we were just far enough from the shore to have been all drowned he became furious, and, plunging desperately, his hind-legs were in the water, then, recovering himself, he beat with such force against the boat-side that we were afraid he should send his feet through. All the while the men were swearing terrible oaths, and cursing the poor beast, redoubling their curses when we reached the landing-place, and whipping him ashore in brutal triumph.

We had only room for half a heartful of joy when we set foot on dry land, for another ferry was to be crossed five miles further. We had intended breakfasting at this house if it had been a decent place; but after this affair we were glad to pay the men off and depart, though I was not well and needed refreshment. The people made us more easy by assuring us that we might easily swim the horse over the next ferry. The first mile or two of our road was over a peat-moss; we then came near to the seashore, and had beautiful views backwards towards the Island of Mull and Dunstaffnage Castle, and forward where the sea ran up between the hills. In this part, on the opposite side of the small bay or elbow of the sea, was a gentleman's house on a hillside, and a building on the hill-top which we took for a lighthouse, but were told that it belonged to the mansion, and was only lighted up on rejoicing days—the laird's birthday, for instance.

Before we had left the peat-moss to travel close to the sea-shore we delighted ourselves with looking on a range of green hills, in shape like those bordering immediately upon the sea, abrupt but not high; they were, in fact, a continuation of the same; but retiring backwards, and rising from the black peat-moss. These hills were of a delicate green, uncommon in Scotland; a foaming rivulet ran down one part, and near it lay two herdsmen full in the sun, with their dogs, among a troop of black cattle which were feeding near, and sprinkled over the whole range of hills—a pastoral scene, to our eyes the more beautiful from knowing what a delightful prospect it must overlook. We now came under the steeps by the sea-side, which were bold rocks, mouldering scars, or fresh with green grass. Under the brow of one of these rocks was a bury-ing-ground, with many upright grave-stones and hay-cocks between, and fenced round by a wall neatly sodded. Near it were one or two houses, with out-houses under a group of trees, but no chapel. The neatness of the burying-ground would in itself have been noticeable in any part of Scotland where we have been; but it was more interesting from its situation than for its own sake—within the sound of the gentlest waves of the sea, and near so many quiet and beautiful objects. There was a range of hills opposite, which we were here first told were the hills of Morven, so much sung of by Ossian. We consulted with some men respecting the ferry, who advised us by all means to send our horse round the loch, and go ourselves over in the boat: they were very civil, and seemed to be intelligent men, yet all disagreed about the length of the loch, though we were not two miles from it: one said it was only six miles long, another ten or fifteen, and afterwards a man whom we met told us it was twenty.

We lost sight of the sea for some time, crossing a half-cultivated space, then reached Loch Creran, a large irregular sea loch, with low sloping banks, coppice woods, and uncultivated grounds, with a scattering of corn fields; as it appeared to us, very thinly inhabited: mountains at a distance. We found only women at home at the ferry-house. I was faint and cold, and went to sit by the fire, but, though very much needing refreshment, I had not heart to eat anything there—the house was so dirty, and there were so many wretchedly dirty women and children; yet perhaps I might have got over the dirt, though I believe there are few ladies who would not have been turned sick by it, if there had not been a most disgusting combination of laziness and coarseness in the countenances and manners of the women, though two of them were very handsome. It was a small hut, and four women were living in it: one, the mother of the children and mistress of the house; the others I supposed to be lodgers, or perhaps servants; but there was no work amongst them. They had just taken from the fire a great pan full of potatoes, which they mixed up with milk, all helping themselves out of the same vessel, and the little children put in their dirty hands to dig out of the mess at their pleasure. I thought to myself, How light the labour of such a house as this! Little sweeping, no washing of floors, and as to scouring the table, I believe it was a thing never thought of.

After a long time the ferryman came home; but we had to wait yet another hour for the tide. In the meanwhile our horse took fright in consequence of his terror at the last ferry, ran away with the car, and dashed out umbrellas, greatcoats, etc.; but luckily he was stopped before any serious mischief was done. We had determined, whatever it cost, not to trust ourselves with him again in the boat; but sending him round the lake seemed almost out of the question, there being no road, and probably much difficulty in going round with a horse; so after some deliberation with the ferryman it was agreed that he should swim over. The usual place of ferrying was very broad, but he was led to the point of a peninsula at a little distance. It being an unusual affair,—indeed, the people of the house said that he was the first horse that had ever swum over,—we had several men on board, and the mistress of the house offered herself as an assistant: we supposed for the sake of a share in eighteen-pennyworth of whisky which her husband called for without ceremony, and of which she and the young lasses, who had helped to push the boat into the water, partook as freely as the men. At first I feared for the horse: he was frightened, and strove to push himself under the boat; but I was soon tolerably easy, for he went on regularly and well, and after from six to ten minutes swimming landed in safety on the other side. Poor creature! he stretched out his nostrils and stared wildly while the man was trotting him about to warm him, and when he put him into the car he was afraid of the sound of the wheels. For some time our road was up a glen, the banks chiefly covered with coppice woods, an unpeopled, but, though without grandeur, not a dreary tract.

Came to a moor and descended into a broad vale, which opened to Loch Linnhe, an arm of the sea, the prospect being shut in by high mountains, on which the sun was shining among mists and resting clouds. A village and chapel stood on the opposite hill; the hills sloped prettily down to the bed of the vale, a large level area—the grounds in general cultivated, but not rich. We went perhaps half a mile down the vale, when our road struck right across it towards the village on the hill-side. We overtook a tall, well-looking man, seemingly about thirty years of age, driving a cart, of whom we inquired concerning the road, and the distance to Portnacroish, our baiting-place. We made further inquiries respecting our future journey, which he answered in an intelligent manner, being perfectly acquainted with the geography of Scotland. He told us that the village which we saw before us and the whole tract of country was called Appin. William said that it was a pretty wild place, to which the man replied, 'Sir, it is a very bonny place if you did but see it on a fine day,' mistaking William's praise for a half-censure; I must say, however, that we hardly ever saw a thoroughly pleasing place in Scotland, which had not something of wildness in its aspect of one sort or other. It came from many causes here: the sea, or sea-loch, of which we only saw as it were a glimpse crossing the vale at the foot of it, the high mountains on the opposite shore, the unenclosed hills on each side of the vale, with black cattle feeding on them, the simplicity of the scattered huts, the half-sheltered, half-exposed situation of the village, the imperfect culture of the fields, the distance from any city or large town, and the very names of Morven and Appin, particularly at such a time, when old Ossian's old friends, sunbeams and mists, as like ghosts as any in the mid-afternoon could be, were keeping company with them. William did all he could to efface the unpleasant impression he had made on the Highlander, and not without success, for he was kind and communicative when we walked up the hill towards the village. He had been a great traveller, in Ireland and elsewhere; but I believe that he had visited no place so beautiful to his eyes as his native home, the strath of Appin under the heathy hills.

We arrived at Portnacroish soon after parting from this man. It is a small village—a few huts and an indifferent inn by the side of the loch. Ordered a fowl for dinner, had a fire lighted, and went a few steps from the door up the road, and turning aside into a field stood at the top of a low eminence, from which, looking down the loch to the sea through a long vista of hills and mountains, we beheld one of the most delightful prospects that, even when we dream of fairer worlds than this, it is possible for us to conceive in our hearts. A covering of clouds rested on the long range of the hills of Morven, mists floated very near to the water on their sides, and were slowly shifting about: yet the sky was clear, and the sea, from the reflection of the sky, of an ethereal or sapphire blue, which was intermingled in many places, and mostly by gentle gradations, with beds of bright dazzling sunshine; green islands lay on the calm water, islands far greener, for so it seemed, than the grass of other places; and from their excessive beauty, their unearthly softness, and the great distance of many of them, they made us think of the islands of the blessed in the Vision of Mirza—a resemblance more striking from the long tract of mist which rested on the top of the steeps of Morven. The view was endless, and though not so wide, had something of the intricacy of the islands and water of Loch Lomond as we saw them from Inch-ta-vanach; and yet how different! At Loch Lomond we could never forget that it was an inland lake of fresh water, nor here that it was the sea itself, though among multitudes of hills. Immediately below us, on an island a few yards from the shore, stood an old keep or fortress; the vale of Appin opened to the water-side, with cultivated fields and cottages. If there were trees near the shore they contributed little to the delightful effect of the scene: it was the immeasurable water, the lofty mist-covered steeps of Morven to the right, the emerald islands without a bush or tree, the celestial colour and brightness of the calm sea, and the innumerable creeks and bays, the communion of land and water as far as the eye could travel. My description must needs be languid; for the sight itself was too fair to be remembered. We sate a long time upon the hill, and pursued our journey at about four o'clock. Had an indifferent dinner, but the cheese was so excellent that William wished to buy the remainder; but the woman would not consent to sell it, and forced us to accept a large portion of it.

We had to travel up the loch, leaving behind us the beautiful scene which we had viewed with such delight before dinner. Often, while we were climbing the hill, did we stop to look back, and when we had gone twenty or thirty yards beyond the point where we had the last view of it, we left the car to the care of some children who were coming from school, and went to take another farewell, always in the hope of bearing away a more substantial remembrance. Travelled for some miles along a road which was so smooth it was more like a gravel walk in a gentleman's grounds than a public highway. Probably the country is indebted for this excellent road to Lord Tweeddale, now a prisoner in France. His house stands upon an eminence within a mile of Portnacroish, commanding the same prospect which I have spoken of, except that it must lose something in not having the old fortress at the foot of it—indeed, it is not to be seen at all from the house or grounds.

We travelled under steep hills, stony or smooth, with coppice-woods and patches of cultivated land, and houses here and there; and at every hundred yards, I may almost venture to say, a streamlet, narrow as a ribbon, came tumbling down, and, crossing our road, fell into the lake below. On the opposite shore, the hills—namely, the continuation of the hills of Morven—were stern and severe, rising like upright walls from the water's edge, and in colour more resembling rocks than hills, as they appeared to us. We did not see any house, or any place where it was likely a house could stand, for many miles; but as the loch was broad we could not perhaps distinguish the objects thoroughly. A little after sunset our road led us from the vale of the loch. We came to a small river, a bridge, a mill, and some cottages at the foot of a hill, and close to the loch.

Did not cross the bridge, but went up the brook, having it on our left, and soon found ourselves in a retired valley, scattered over with many grey huts, and surrounded on every side by green hills. The hay grounds in the middle of the vale were unenclosed, which was enough to keep alive the Scottish wildness, here blended with exceeding beauty; for there were trees growing irregularly or in clumps all through the valley, rocks or stones here and there, which, with the people at work, hay-cocks sprinkled over the fields, made the vale look full and populous. It was a sweet time of the evening: the moon was up; but there was yet so much of day that her light was not perceived. Our road was through open fields; the people suspended their work as we passed along, and leaning on their pitchforks or rakes, with their arms at their sides, or hanging down, some in one way, some in another, and no two alike, they formed most beautiful groups, the outlines of their figures being much more distinct than by day, and all that might have been harsh or unlovely softened down. The dogs were, as usual, attendant on their masters, and, watching after us, they barked aloud; yet even their barking hardly disturbed the quiet of the place.

I cannot say how long this vale was; it made the larger half of a circle, or a curve deeper than that of half a circle, before it opened again upon the loch. It was less thoroughly cultivated and woody after the last turning—the hills steep and lofty. We met a very tall stout man, a fine figure, in a Highland bonnet, with a little girl, driving home their cow: he accosted us, saying that we were late travellers, and that we had yet four miles to go before we should reach Ballachulish—a long way, uncertain as we were respecting our accommodations. He told us that the vale was called the Strath of Duror, and when we said it was a pretty place, he answered, Indeed it was, and that they lived very comfortably there, for they had a good master, Lord Tweed-dale, whose imprisonment he lamented, speaking earnestly of his excellent qualities. At the end of the vale we came close upon a large bay of the loch, formed by a rocky hill, a continuation of the ridge of high hills on the left side of the strath, making a very grand promontory, under which was a hamlet, a cluster of huts, at the water's edge, with their little fleet of fishing boats at anchor, and behind, among the rocks, a hundred slips of corn, slips and patches, often no bigger than a garden such as a child, eight years old, would make for sport: it might have been the work of a small colony from China. There was something touching to the heart in this appearance of scrupulous industry, and excessive labour of the soil, in a country where hills and mountains, and even valleys, are left to the care of nature and the pleasure of the cattle that feed among them. It was, indeed, a very interesting place, the more so being in perfect contrast with the few houses at the entrance of the strath—a sea hamlet, without trees, under a naked stony mountain, yet perfectly sheltered, standing in the middle of a large bay which half the winds that travel over the lake can never visit. The other, a little bowery spot, with its river, bridge, and mill, might have been a hundred miles from the sea-side.

The moon was now shining, and though it reminded us how far the evening was advanced, we stopped for many minutes before we could resolve to go on; we saw nothing stirring, neither men, women, nor cattle; but the linen was still bleaching by the stony rivulet, which ran near the houses in water-breaks and tiny cataracts. For the first half mile after we had left this scene there was no thing remarkable; and afterwards we could only see the hills, the sky, the moon, and moonlight water. When we came within, it might be, half a mile of Ballachulish, the place where we were to lodge, the loch narrowed very much, the hills still continuing high. I speak inaccurately, for it split into two divisions, the one along which we went being called Loch Leven.

The road grew very bad, and we had an anxious journey till we saw a light before us, which with great joy we assured ourselves was from the inn; but what was our distress when, on going a few steps further, we came to a bridge half broken down, with bushes laid across to prevent travellers from going over. After some perplexity we determined that I should walk on to the house before us—for we could see that the bridge was safe for foot-passengers—and ask for assistance. By great good luck, at this very moment four or five men came along the road towards us and offered to help William in driving the car through the water, which was not very deep at that time, though, only a few days before, the damage had been done to the bridge by a flood.

I walked on to the inn, ordered tea, and was conducted into a lodging room. I desired to have a fire, and was answered with the old scruple about 'giving fire,'—with, at the same time, an excuse 'that it was so late,'—the girl, however, would ask the landlady, who was lying-in; the fire was brought immediately, and from that time the girl was very civil. I was not, however, quite at ease, for William stayed long, and I was going to leave my fire to seek after him, when I heard him at the door with the horse and car. The horse had taken fright with the roughness of the river-bed and the rattling of the wheels—the second fright in consequence of the ferry—and the men had been obliged to unyoke him and drag the car through, a troublesome affair for William; but he talked less of the trouble and alarm than of the pleasure he had felt in having met with such true good-will and ready kindness in the Highlanders. They drank their glass of whisky at the door, wishing William twenty good wishes, and asking him twice as many questions,—if he was married, if he had an estate, where he lived, etc. etc. This inn is the ferry-house on the main road up into the Highlands by Fort-William, and here Coleridge, though unknown to us, had slept three nights before.

Saturday, September 3d.—When we have arrived at an unknown place by moonlight, it is never a moment of indifference when I quit it again with the morning light, especially if the objects have appeared beautiful, or in any other way impressive or interesting. I have kept back, unwilling to go to the window, that I might not lose the picture taken to my pillow at night. So it was at Ballachulish: and instantly I felt that the passing away of my own fancies was a loss. The place had appeared exceedingly wild by moonlight; I had mistaken corn-fields for naked rocks, and the lake had appeared narrower and the hills more steep and lofty than they really were.

We rose at six o'clock, and took a basin of milk before we set forward on our journey to Glen Coe. It was a delightful morning, the road excellent, and we were in good spirits, happy that we had no more ferries to cross, and pleased with the thought that we were going among the grand mountains which we saw before us at the head of the loch. We travelled close to the water's edge, and were rolling along a smooth road, when the horse suddenly backed, frightened by the upright shafts of a roller rising from behind the wall of a field adjoining the road. William pulled, whipped, and struggled in vain; we both leapt upon the ground, and the horse dragged the car after him, he going backwards down the bank of the loch, and it was turned over, half in the water, the horse lying on his back, struggling in the harness, a frightful sight! I gave up everything; thought that the horse would be lamed, and the car broken to pieces. Luckily a man came up in the same moment, and assisted William in extricating the horse, and, after an hour's delay, with the help of strings and pocket-handkerchiefs, we mended the harness and set forward again, William leading the poor animal all the way, for the regular beating of the waves frightened him, and any little gushing stream that crossed the road would have sent him off. The village where the blacksmith lived was before us—a few huts under the mountains, and, as it seemed, at the head of the loch; but it runs further up to the left, being narrowed by a hill above the village, near which, at the edge of the water, was a slate quarry, and many large boats with masts, on the water below, high mountains shutting in the prospect, which stood in single, distinguishable shapes, yet clustered together—simple and bold in their forms, and their surfaces of all characters and all colours—some that looked as if scarified by fire, others green; and there was one that might have been blasted by an eternal frost, its summit and sides for a considerable way down being as white as hoar-frost at eight o'clock on a winter's morning. No clouds were on the hills; the sun shone bright, but the wind blew fresh and cold.

When we reached the blacksmith's shop, I left William to help to take care of the horse, and went into the house. The mistress, with a child in her arms and two or three running about, received me very kindly, making many apologies for the dirty house, which she partly attributed to its being Saturday; but I could plainly see that it was dirt of all days. I sate in the midst of it with great delight, for the woman's benevolent, happy countenance almost converted her slovenly and lazy way of leaving all things to take care of themselves into a comfort and a blessing.

It was not a Highland hut, but a slated house built by the master of the quarry for the accommodation of his black-smith,—the shell of an English cottage, as if left unfinished by the workmen, without plaster, and with floor of mud. Two beds, with not over-clean bedclothes, were in the room. Luckily for me, there was a good fire and a boiling kettle. The woman was very sorry she had no butter; none was to be had in the village: she gave me oaten and barley bread. We talked over the fire; I answered her hundred questions, and in my turn put some to her. She asked me, as usual, if I was married, how many brothers I had, etc. etc. I told her that William was married, and had a fine boy; to which she replied, 'And the man's a decent man too.' Her next-door neighbour came in with a baby on her arm, to request that I would accept of some fish, which I broiled in the ashes. She joined in our conversation, but with more shyness than her neighbour, being a very young woman. She happened to say that she was a stranger in that place, and had been bred and born a long way off. On my asking her where, she replied, 'At Leadhills;' and when I told her that I had been there, a joy lighted up her countenance which I shall never forget, and when she heard that it was only a fortnight before, her eyes filled with tears. I was exceedingly affected with the simplicity of her manners; her tongue was now let loose, and she would have talked for ever of Leadhills, of her mother, of the quietness of the people in general, and the goodness of Mrs. Otto, who, she told me, was a 'varra discreet woman.' She was sure we should be 'well put up' at Mrs. Otto's, and praised her house and furniture; indeed, it seemed she thought all earthly comforts were gathered together under the bleak heights that surround the villages of Wanlockhead and Leadhills: and afterwards, when I said it was a wild country thereabouts, she even seemed surprised, and said it was not half so wild as where she lived now. One circumstance which she mentioned of Mrs. Otto I must record, both in proof of her 'discretion,' and the sobriety of the people at Leadhills, namely, that no liquor was ever drunk in her house after a certain hour of the night—I have forgotten what hour; but it was an early one, I am sure not later than ten.

The blacksmith, who had come in to his breakfast, was impatient to finish our job, that he might go out into the hay-field, for, it being a fine day, every plot of hay-ground was scattered over with hay-makers. On my saying that I guessed much of their hay must be spoiled, he told me no, for that they had high winds, which dried it quickly,—the people understood the climate, 'were clever at the work, and got it in with a blink.' He hastily swallowed his breakfast, dry bread and a basin of weak tea without sugar, and held his baby on his knee till he had done.

The women and I were again left to the fireside, and there were no limits to their joy in me, for they discovered another bond of connexion. I lived in the same part of England from which Mr. Rose, the superintendent of the slate-quarries, and his wife, had come. 'Oh!' said Mrs. Stuart—so her neighbour called her, they not giving each other their Christian names, as is common in Cumberland and Westmoreland,—'Oh!' said she, 'what would not I give to see anybody that came from within four or five miles of Leadhills?' They both exclaimed that I must see Mrs. Rose; she would make much of me—she would have given me tea and bread and butter and a good breakfast. I learned from the two women, Mrs. Stuart and Mrs. Duncan—so the other was called—that Stuart had come from Leadhills for the sake of better wages, to take the place of Duncan, who had resigned his office of blacksmith to the quarries, as far as I could learn, in a pet, intending to go to America, that his wife was averse to go, and that the scheme, for this cause and through other difficulties, had been given up. He appeared to be a good-tempered man, and made us a most reasonable charge for mending the car. His wife told me that they must give up the house in a short time to the other blacksmith; she did not know whither they should go, but her husband, being a good workman, could find employment anywhere. She hurried me out to introduce me to Mrs. Rose, who was at work in the hay-field; she was exceedingly glad to see one of her country-women, and entreated that I would go up to her house. It was a substantial plain house, that would have held half-a-dozen of the common huts. She conducted me into a sitting-room up-stairs, and set before me red and white wine, with the remnant of a loaf of wheaten bread, which she took out of a cupboard in the sitting-room, and some delicious butter. She was a healthy and cheerful-looking woman, dressed like one of our country lasses, and had certainly had no better education than Aggy Ashburner, but she was as a chief in this secluded place, a Madam of the village, and seemed to be treated with the utmost respect.

In our way to and from the house we met several people who interchanged friendly greetings with her, but always as with one greatly superior. She attended me back to the blacksmith's, and would not leave me till she had seen us set forward again on our journey. Mrs. Duncan and Mrs. Stuart shook me cordially, nay, affectionately, by the hand. I tried to prevail upon the former, who had been my hostess, to accept of some money, but in vain; she would not take a farthing, and though I told her it was only to buy something for her little daughter, even seemed grieved that I should think it possible. I forgot to mention that while the blacksmith was repairing the car, we walked to the slate-quarry, where we saw again some of the kind creatures who had helped us in our difficulties the night before. The hovel under which they split their slates stood upon an out-jutting rock, a part of the quarry rising immediately out of the water, and commanded a fine prospect down the loch below Ballachulish, and upwards towards the grand mountains, and the other horn of the vale where the lake was concealed. The blacksmith drove our car about a mile of the road; we then hired a man and horse to take me and the car to the top of Glen Coe, being afraid that if the horse backed or took fright we might be thrown down some precipice.

But before we departed we could not resist our inclination to climb up the hill which I have mentioned as appearing to terminate the loch. The mountains, though inferior to those of Glen Coe, on the other side are very majestic; and the solitude in which we knew the unseen lake was bedded at their feet was enough to excite our longings. We climbed steep after steep, far higher than they appeared to us, and I was going to give up the accomplishment of our aim, when a glorious sight on the mountain before us made me forget my fatigue. A slight shower had come on, its skirts falling upon us, and half the opposite side of the mountain was wrapped up in rainbow light, covered as by a veil with one dilated rainbow: so it continued for some minutes;

and the shower and rainy clouds passed away as suddenly as they had come, and the sun shone again upon the tops of all the hills. In the meantime we reached the wished-for point, and saw to the head of the loch. Perhaps it might not be so beautiful as we had imaged it in our thoughts, but it was beautiful enough not to disappoint us,—a narrow deep valley, a perfect solitude, without house or hut. One of the hills was thinly sprinkled with Scotch firs, which appeared to be the survivors of a large forest: they were the first natural wild Scotch firs we had seen. Though thinned of their numbers, and left, comparatively, to a helpless struggle with the elements, we were much struck with the gloom, and even grandeur, of the trees.

Hastened back again to join the car, but were tempted to go a little out of our way to look at a nice white house belonging to the laird of Glen Coe, which stood sweetly in a green field under the hill near some tall trees and coppice woods. At this house the horrible massacre of Glen Coe began, which we did not know when we were there; but the house must have been rebuilt since that time. We had a delightful walk through fields, among copses, and by a river-side: we could have fancied ourselves in some part of the north of England unseen before, it was so much like it, and yet so different. I must not forget one place on the opposite side of the water, where we longed to live—a snug white house on the mountain-side, surrounded by its own green fields and woods, the high mountain above, the loch below, and inaccessible but by means of boats. A beautiful spot indeed it was; but in the retired parts of Scotland a comfortable white house is itself such a pleasant sight, that I believe, without our knowing how or why, it makes us look with a more loving eye on the fields and trees than for their own sakes they deserve.

At about one o'clock we set off, William on our own horse, and I with my Highland driver. He was perfectly acquainted with the country, being a sort of carrier or carrier-merchant or shopkeeper, going frequently to Glasgow with his horse and cart to fetch and carry goods and merchandise. He knew the name of every hill, almost every rock; and I made good use of his knowledge; but partly from laziness, and still more because it was inconvenient, I took no notes, and now I am little better for what he told me. He spoke English tolerably; but seldom understood what was said to him without a 'What's your wull?' We turned up to the right, and were at the foot of the glen—the laird's house cannot be said to be *in* the glen. The afternoon was delightful,—the sun shone, the mountain-tops were clear, the lake glittered in the great vale behind us, and the stream of Glen Coe flowed down to it glittering among alder-trees. The meadows of the glen were of the freshest green; one new-built stone house in the first reach, some huts, hillocks covered with wood, alder-trees scattered all over. Looking backward, we were reminded of Patterdale and the head of Ulswater, but forward the greatness of the mountains overcame every other idea.

The impression was, as we advanced up to the head of this first reach, as if the glen were nothing, its loneliness and retirement—as if it made up no part of my feeling: the mountains were all in all. That which fronted us—I have forgotten its name—was exceedingly lofty, the surface stony, nay, the whole mountain was one mass of stone, wrinkled and puckered up together. At the second and last reach—for it is not a winding vale—it makes a quick turning almost at right angles to the first; and now we are in the depths of the mountains; no trees in the glen, only green pasturage for sheep, and here and there a plot of hay-ground, and something that tells of former cultivation. I observed this to the guide, who said that formerly the glen had had many inhabitants, and that there, as elsewhere in the Highlands, there had been a great deal of corn where now the lands were left waste, and nothing fed upon them but cattle. I cannot attempt to describe the mountains. I can only say that I thought those on our right—for the other side was only a continued high ridge or craggy barrier, broken along the top into petty spiral forms—were the grandest I had ever seen. It seldom happens that mountains in a very clear air look exceedingly high, but these, though we could see the whole of them to their very summits, appeared to me more majestic in their own nakedness than our imaginations could have conceived them to be, had they been half hidden by clouds, yet showing some of their highest pinnacles. They were such forms as Milton might be supposed to have had in his mind when he applied to Satan that sublime expression—

'His stature reached the sky.'

The first division of the glen, as I have said, was scattered over with rocks, trees, and woody hillocks, and cottages were to be seen here and there. The second division is bare and stony, huge mountains on all sides, with a slender pasturage in the bottom of the valley; and towards the head of it is a small lake or tarn, and near the tarn a single inhabited dwelling, and some unfenced hay-ground—a simple impressive scene! Our road frequently crossed large streams of stones, left by the mountain-torrents, losing all appearance of a road. After we had passed the tarn the glen became less interesting, or rather the mountains, from the manner in which they are looked at; but again, a little higher up, they resume their grandeur. The river is, for a short space, hidden between steep rocks: we left the road, and, going to the top of one of the rocks, saw it foaming over stones, or lodged in dark black dens; birch-trees grew on the inaccessible banks, and a few old Scotch firs towered above them. At the entrance of the glen the mountains had been all without trees, but here the birches climb very far up the side of one of them opposite to us, half concealing a rivulet, which came tumbling down as white as snow from the very top of the mountain. Leaving the rock, we ascended a hill which terminated the glen. We often stopped to look behind at the majestic company of mountains we had left. Before us was no single paramount eminence, but a mountain waste, mountain beyond mountain, and a barren hollow or basin into which we were descending.

We parted from our companion at the door of a whisky hovel, a building which, when it came out of the workmen's hands with its unglassed windows, would, in that forlorn region, have been little better than a howling place for the winds, and was now half unroofed. On seeing a smoke, I exclaimed, 'Is it possible any people can live there?' when at least half a dozen, men, women, and children, came to the door. They were about to rebuild the hut, and I suppose that they, or some other poor creatures, would dwell there through the winter, dealing out whisky to the starved travellers. The sun was now setting, the air very cold, the sky clear; I could have fancied that it was winter-time, with hard frost. Our guide pointed out King's House to us, our resting-place for the night. We could just distinguish the house at the bottom of the moorish hollow or basin—I call it so, for it was nearly as broad as long—lying before us, with three miles of naked road winding through it, every foot of which we could see. The road was perfectly white, making a dreary contrast with the ground, which was of a dull earthy brown. Long as the line of road appeared before us, we could scarcely believe it to be three miles—I suppose owing to its being unbroken by any one object, and the moor naked as the road itself, but we found it the longest three miles we had yet travelled, for the surface was so stony we had to walk most of the way.

The house looked respectable at a distance—a large square building, cased in blue slates to defend it from storms,—but when we came close to it the outside forewarned us of the poverty and misery within. Scarce a blade of grass could be seen growing upon the open ground; the heath-plant itself found no nourishment there, appearing as if it had but sprung up to be blighted. There was no enclosure for a cow, no appropriated ground but a small plot like a church yard, in which were a few starveling dwarfish potatoes, which had, no doubt, been raised by means of the dung left by travellers' horses: they had not come to blossoming, and whether they would either yield fruit or blossom I know not. The first thing we saw on entering the door was two sheep hung up, as if just killed from the barren moor, their bones hardly sheathed in flesh. After we had waited a few minutes, looking about for a guide to lead us into some corner of the house, a woman, seemingly about forty years old, came to us in a great bustle, screaming in Erse, with the most horrible guinea-hen or peacock voice I ever heard, first to one person, then another. She could hardly spare time to show us up-stairs, for crowds of men were in the house—drovers, carriers, horsemen, travellers, all of whom she had to provide with supper, and she was, as she told us, the only woman there.

Never did I see such a miserable, such a wretched place,—long rooms with ranges of beds, no other furniture except benches, or perhaps one or two crazy chairs, the floors far dirtier than an ordinary house could be if it were never washed,—as dirty as a house after a sale on a rainy day, and the rooms being large, and the walls naked, they looked as if more than half the goods had been sold out. We sate shivering in one of the large rooms for three quarters of an hour before the woman could find time to speak to us again; she then promised a fire in another room, after two travellers, who were going a stage further, had finished their whisky, and said we should have supper as soon as possible. She had no eggs, no milk, no potatoes, no loaf-bread, or we should have preferred tea. With length of time the fire was kindled, and, after another hour's waiting, supper came,—a shoulder of mutton so hard that it was impossible to chew the little flesh that might be scraped off the bones, and some sorry soup made of barley and water, for it had no other taste.

After supper, the woman, having first asked if we slept on blankets, brought in two pair of sheets, which she begged that I would air by the fire, for they would be dirtied below-stairs. I was very willing, but behold! the sheets were so wet, that it would have been at least a two-hours' job before a far better fire than could be mustered at King's House,—for, that nothing might be wanting to make it a place of complete starvation, the peats were not dry, and if they had not been helped out by decayed wood dug out of the earth along with them, we should have had no fire at all. The woman was civil, in her fierce, wild way. She and the house, upon that desolate and extensive Wild, and everything we saw, made us think of one of those places of rendezvous which we read of in novels— Ferdinand Count Fathom, or Gil Blas,—where there is one woman to receive the booty, and prepare the supper at night. She told us that she was only a servant, but that she had now lived there five years, and that, when but a 'young lassie,' she had lived there also. We asked her if she had always served the same master, 'Nay, nay, many masters, for they were always changing.' I verily believe that the woman was attached to the place like a cat to the empty house when the family who brought her up are gone to live elsewhere. The sheets were so long in drying that it was very late before we went to bed. We talked over our day's adventures by the fireside, and often looked out of the window towards a huge pyramidal mountain at the entrance of Glen Coe. All between, the dreary waste was clear, almost, as sky, the moon shining full upon it. A rivulet ran amongst stones near the house, and sparkled with light: I could have fancied that there was nothing else, in that extensive circuit over which we looked, that had the power of motion.

In comparing the impressions we had received at Glen Coe, we found that though the expectations of both had been far surpassed by the grandeur of the mountains, we had upon the whole both been disappointed, and from the same cause: we had been prepared for images of terror, had expected a deep, den-like valley with overhanging rocks, such as William has described in these lines, speaking of the Alps:—

> Brook and road
> Were fellow-travellers in this gloomy Pass,
> And with them did we journey several hours
> At a slow step. The immeasurable height
> Of woods decaying, never to be decayed!
> The stationary blasts of waterfalls;
> And everywhere along the hollow rent
> Winds thwarting winds, bewilder'd and forlorn;
> The torrents shooting from the clear blue sky,
> The rocks that mutter'd close upon our ears,
> Black drizzling crags that spake by the way-side
> As if a voice were in them; the sick sight

And giddy prospect of the raving stream;
The unfetter'd clouds, and region of the heavens,
Tumult and peace, the darkness and the light,
Were all like workings of one mind, the features
Of the same face, blossoms upon one tree,
Characters of the great Apocalypse,
The Types and Symbols of Eternity,
Of first, and last, and midst, and without end.

The place had nothing of this character, the glen being open to the eye of day, the mountains retiring in independent majesty. Even in the upper part of it, where the stream rushed through the rocky chasm, it was but a deep trench in the vale, not the vale itself, and could only be seen when we were close to it.

Fourth Week.

Sunday, September 4th. — We had desired to be called at six o'clock, and rose at the first summons. Our beds had proved better than we expected, and we had not slept ill; but poor Coleridge had passed a wretched night here four days before. This we did not know; but since, when he told us of it, the notion of what he must have suffered, with the noise of drunken people about his ears all night, himself sick and tired, has made our discomfort cling to my memory, and given these recollections a twofold interest. I asked if it was possible to have a couple of eggs boiled before our departure: the woman hesitated; she thought I might, and sent a boy into the out-houses to look about, who brought in one egg after long searching. Early as we had risen it was not very early when we set off; for everything at King's House was in unison—equally uncomfortable. As the woman had told us the night before, 'They had no hay, and that was a loss.' There were neither stalls nor bedding in the stable, so that William was obliged to watch the horse while it was feeding, for there were several others in the stable, all standing like wild beasts, ready to devour each other's portion of corn: this, with the slowness of the servant and other hindrances, took up much time, and we were completely starved, for the morning was very cold, as I believe all the mornings in that desolate place are.

When we had gone about a quarter of a mile I recollected that I had left the little cup given me by the kind landlady at Taynuilt, which I had intended that John should hereafter drink out of, in memory of our wanderings. I would have turned back for it, but William pushed me on, unwilling that we should lose so much time, though indeed he was as sorry to part with it as myself.

Our road was over a hill called the Black Mount. For the first mile, or perhaps more, after we left King's House, we ascended on foot; then came upon a new road, one of the finest that was ever trod; and, as we went downwards almost all the way afterwards, we travelled very quickly. The motion was pleasant, the different reaches and windings of the road were amusing; the sun shone, the mountain-tops were clear and cheerful, and we in good spirits, in a bustle of enjoyment, though there never was a more desolate region: mountains behind, before, and on every side; I do not remember to have seen either patch of grass, flower, or flowering heather within three or four miles of King's House. The low ground was not rocky, but black, and full of white frost-bleached stones, the prospect only varied by pools, seen everywhere both near and at a distance, as far as the ground stretched out below us: these were interesting spots, round which the mind assembled living objects, and they shone as bright as mirrors in the forlorn waste. We passed neither tree nor shrub for miles—I include the whole space from Glen Coe—yet we saw perpetually traces of a long decayed forest, pieces of black mouldering wood.

Through such a country as this we had travelled perhaps seven and a half miles this morning, when, after descending a hill, we turned to the right, and saw an unexpected sight in the moorland hollow into which we were entering, a small lake bounded on the opposite side by a grove of Scotch firs, two or three cottages at the head of it, and a lot of cultivated ground with scattered hay-cocks. The road along which we were going, after having made a curve considerably above the tarn, was seen winding through the trees on the other side, a beautiful object, and, luckily for us, a drove of cattle happened to be passing there at the very time, a stream coursing the road, with off-stragglers to the borders of the lake, and under the trees on the sloping ground.

In conning over our many wanderings I shall never forget the gentle pleasure with which we greeted the lake of Inveroran and its few grey cottages: we suffered our horse to slacken his pace, having now no need of the comfort of quick motion, though we were glad to think that one of those cottages might be the public-house where we were to breakfast. A forest—now, as it appeared, dwindled into the small grove bordering the lake—had, not many years ago, spread to that side of the vale where we were: large stumps of trees which had been cut down were yet remaining undecayed, and there were some single trees left alive, as if by their battered black boughs to tell us of the storms that visit the valley which looked now so sober and peaceful. When we arrived at the huts, one of them proved to be the inn, a thatched house without a sign-board. We were kindly received, had a fire lighted in the parlour, and were in such good humour that we seemed to have a thousand comforts about us; but we had need of a little patience in addition to this good humour before breakfast was brought, and at last it proved a disappointment: the butter not eatable, the barley-cakes fusty, the oat-bread so hard I could not chew it, and there were only four eggs in the house, which they had boiled as hard as stones.

Before we had finished breakfast two foot-travellers came in, and seated themselves at our table; one of them was returning, after a long absence, to Fort-William, his native home; he had come from Egypt, and, many years ago, had been on a recruiting party at Penrith, and knew many people there. He seemed to think his own country but a dismal land.

There being no bell in the parlour, I had occasion to go several times and ask for what we wanted in the kitchen, and I would willingly have given twenty pounds to have been able to take a lively picture of it. About seven or eight travellers, probably drovers, with as many dogs, were sitting in a complete circle round a large peat-fire in the middle of the floor, each with a mess of porridge, in a wooden vessel, upon his knee; a pot, suspended from one of the black beams, was boiling on the fire; two or three women pursuing their household business on the outside of the circle, children playing on the floor. There was nothing uncomfortable in this confusion: happy, busy, or vacant faces, all looked pleasant; and even the smoky air, being a sort of natural indoor atmosphere of Scotland, served only to give a softening, I may say harmony, to the whole.

We departed immediately after breakfast; our road leading us, as I have said, near the lake-side and through the grove of firs, which extended backward much further than we had imagined. After we had left it we came again among bare moorish wastes, as before, under the mountains, so that Inveroran still lives in our recollection as a favoured place, a flower in the desert.

Descended upon the whole, I believe very considerably, in our way to Tyndrum; but it was a road of long ups and downs, over hills and through hollows of uncultivated ground; a chance farm perhaps once in three miles, a glittering rivulet bordered with greener grass than grew on the broad waste, or a broken fringe of alders or birches, partly concealing and partly pointing out its course.

Arrived at Tyndrum at about two o'clock. It is a cold spot. Though, as I should suppose, situated lower than Inveroran, and though we saw it in the hottest time of the afternoon sun, it had a far colder aspect from the want of trees. We were here informed that Coleridge, who, we supposed, was gone to Edinburgh, had dined at this very house a few days before, in his road to Fort-William. By the help of the cook, who was called in, the landlady made out the very day: it was the day after we parted from him; as she expressed it, the day after the 'great speet,' namely, the great rain. We had a moorfowl and mutton-chops for dinner, well cooked, and a reasonable charge. The house was clean for a Scotch inn, and the people about the doors were well dressed. In one of the parlours we saw a company of nine or ten, with the landlady, seated round a plentiful table,—a sight which made us think of the fatted calf in the alehouse pictures of the Prodigal Son. There seemed to be a whole harvest of meats and drinks, and there was something of festivity and picture-like gaiety even in the fresh-coloured dresses of the people and their Sunday faces. The white table-cloth, glasses, English dishes, etc., were all in contrast with what we had seen at Inveroran: the places were but about nine miles asunder, both among hills; the rank of the people little different, and each house appeared to be a house of plenty.

We were I think better pleased with our treatment at this inn than any of the lonely houses on the road, except Taynuilt; but Coleridge had not fared so well, and was dissatisfied, as he has since told us, and the two travellers who breakfasted with us at Inveroran had given a bad account of the house.

Left Tyndrum at about five o'clock; a gladsome afternoon; the road excellent, and we bowled downwards through a pleasant vale, though not populous, or well cultivated, or woody, but enlivened by a river that glittered as it flowed. On the side of a sunny hill a knot of men and women were gathered together at a preaching. We passed by many droves of cattle and Shetland ponies, which accident stamped a character upon places, else unrememberable—not an individual character, but the soul, the spirit, and solitary simplicity of many a Highland region.

We had about eleven miles to travel before we came to our lodging, and had gone five or six, almost always descending, and still in the same vale, when we saw a small lake before us after the vale had made a bending to the left; it was about sunset when we came up to the lake; the afternoon breezes had died away, and the water was in perfect stillness. One grove-like island, with a ruin that stood upon it overshadowed by the trees, was reflected on the water. This building, which, on that beautiful evening, seemed to be wrapped up in religious quiet, we were informed had been raised for defence by some Highland chieftain. All traces of strength, or war, or danger are passed away, and in the mood in which we were we could only look upon it as a place of retirement and peace. The lake is called Loch Dochart. We passed by two others of inferior beauty, and continued to travel along the side of the same river, the Dochart, through an irregular, undetermined vale,—poor soil and much waste land.

At that time of the evening when, by looking steadily, we could discover a few pale stars in the sky, we saw upon an eminence, the bound of our horizon, though very near to us, and facing the bright yellow clouds of the west, a group of figures that made us feel how much we wanted in not being painters. Two herdsmen, with a dog beside them, were sitting on the hill, overlooking a herd of cattle scattered over a large meadow by the river-side. Their forms, looked at through a fading light, and backed by the bright west, were exceedingly distinct, a beautiful picture in the quiet of a Sabbath evening, exciting thoughts and images of almost patriarchal simplicity and grace. We were much pleased with the situation of our inn, where we arrived between eight and nine o'clock. The river was at the distance of a broad field from the door; we could see it from the upper windows and hear its murmuring; the moon shone, enlivening the large corn fields with cheerful light. We had a bad supper, and the next morning they made us an unreasonable charge; and the servant was uncivil, because, forsooth! we had no wine.

N.B.—The travellers in the morning had spoken highly of this inn.

Monday, September 5th.—After drinking a bason of milk we set off again at a little after six o'clock—a fine morning—eight miles to Killin—the river Dochart always on our left. The face of the country not very interesting, though not unpleasing, reminding us of some of the vales of the north of England, though meagre, nipped-up, or shrivelled compared with them. There were rocks, and rocky knolls, as about Grasmere and Wytheburn, and copses, but of a starveling growth; the cultivated ground poor. Within a mile or two of Killin the land was better cultivated, and, looking down the vale, we had a view of Loch Tay, into which the Dochart falls. Close to the town, the river took up a roaring voice, beating its way over a rocky descent among large black stones: islands in the middle turning the stream this way and that; the whole course of the river very wide. We crossed it by means of three bridges, which make one continued bridge of a great length. On an island below the bridge is a gateway with tall pillars, leading to an old bury-ing-ground belonging to some noble family. It has a singular appearance, and the place is altogether uncommon and romantic—a remnant of ancient grandeur: extreme natural wildness—the sound of roaring water, and withal, the ordi-nary half-village, half-town bustle of an every-day place.

The inn at Killin is one of the largest on the Scotch road: it stands pleasantly, near the chapel, at some distance from the river Dochart, and out of reach of its tumultuous noise; and another broad, stately, and silent stream, which you cannot look at without remembering its boisterous neigh-bour, flows close under the windows of the inn, and beside the churchyard, in which are many graves. That river falls into the lake at the distance of nearly a mile from the mouth of the Dochart. It is bordered with tall trees and corn fields, bearing plentiful crops, the richest we had seen in Scotland.

After breakfast we walked onwards, expecting that the stream would lead us into some considerable vale; but it soon became little better than a common rivulet, and the glen appeared to be short; indeed, we wondered how the river had grown so great all at once. Our horse had not been able to eat his corn, and we waited a long time in the hope that he would be better. At eleven o'clock, however, we determined to set off, and give him all the ease possible by walking up the hills, and not pushing beyond a slow walk. We had fourteen miles to travel to Kenmore, by the side of Loch Tay. Crossed the same bridge again, and went down the south side of the lake. We had a delightful view of the village of Killin, among rich green fields, corn and wood, and up towards the two horns of the vale of Tay, the valley of the Dochart, and the other valley with its full-grown river, the prospect terminated by mountains. We travelled through lanes, woods, or open fields, never close to the lake, but always near it, for many miles, the road being carried along the side of a hill, which rose in an almost regularly receding steep from the lake. The opposite shore did not much differ from that down which we went, but it seemed more thinly inhabited, and not so well culti-vated. The sun shone, the cottages were pleasant, and the goings-on of the harvest—for all the inhabitants were at work in the corn fields—made the way cheerful. But there is an uniformity in the lake which, comparing it with other lakes, made it appear tiresome. It has no windings: I should even imagine, although it is so many miles long, that, from some points not very high on the hills, it may be seen from one end to the other. There are few bays, no lurking-places where the water hides itself in the land, no outjutting points or promontories, no islands; and there are no commanding mountains or precipices. I think that this lake would be the most pleasing in spring-time, or in summer before the corn begins to change colour, the long tracts of hills on each side of the vale having at this season a kind of patchy appearance, for the corn fields in general were very small, mere plots, and of every possible shade of bright yellow. When we came in view of the foot of the lake we perceived that it ended, as it had begun, in pride and loveliness. The village of Kenmore, with its neat church and cleanly houses, stands on a gentle eminence at the end of the water. The view, though not near so beautiful as that of Killin, is exceedingly pleasing. Left our car, and turned out of the road at about the distance of a mile from the town, and after having climbed perhaps a quarter of a mile, we were conducted into a locked-up plantation, and guessed by the sound that we were near the cascade, but could not see it. Our guide opened a door, and we entered a dungeon-like passage, and, after walking some yards in total darkness, found ourselves in a quaint apartment stuck over with moss, hung about with stuffed foxes and other wild animals, and ornamented with a library of wooden books covered with old leather backs, the mock furniture of a hermit's cell. At the end of the room, through a large bow-window, we saw the waterfall, and at the same time, looking down to the left, the village of Kenmore and a part of the lake—a very beautiful prospect.

William Wordsworth

Stepping Westward

"*What, you are stepping westward?*"—"*Yea.*"
   'Twould be a *wildish* destiny,
If we, who thus together roam
In a strange Land, and far from home,
Were in this place the guests of Chance:
Yet who would stop, or fear to advance,
Though home or shelter he had none,
With such a sky to lead him on?

The dewy ground was dark and cold;
Behind, all gloomy to behold;
And stepping westward seemed to be
A kind of *heavenly* destiny:
I liked the greeting; 'twas a sound
Of something without place or bound;
And seemed to give me spiritual right
To travel through that region bright.

The voice was soft, and she who spake
Was walking by her native lake:
The salutation had to me
The very sound of courtesy:
Its power was felt; and while my eye
Was fixed upon the glowing Sky,
The echo of the voice enwrought
A human sweetness with the thought
Of travelling through the world that lay
Before me in my endless way.

The Solitary Reaper

Behold her, single in the field,
Yon solitary Highland Lass!
Reaping and singing by herself;
Stop here, or gently pass!
Alone she cuts and binds the grain,
And sings a melancholy strain;
O listen! for the Vale profound
Is overflowing with the sound.

No Nightingale did ever chaunt
More welcome notes to weary bands
Of travellers in some shady haunt,
Among Arabian sands:
A voice so thrilling ne'er was heard
In spring-time from the Cuckoo-bird,
Breaking the silence of the seas
Among the farthest Hebrides.

Will no one tell me what she sings?—
Perhaps the plaintive numbers flow
For old, unhappy, far-off things,
And battles long ago:

Or is it some more humble lay,
Familiar matter of to-day?
Some natural sorrow, loss, or pain,
That has been, and may be again?

Whate'er the theme, the Maiden sang
As if her song could have no ending;
I saw her singing at her work,
And o'er the sickle bending;—
I listened, motionless and still;
And, as I mounted up the hill,
The music in my heart I bore,
Long after it was heard no more.

To the Cuckoo

O blithe New-comer! I have heard,
I hear thee and rejoice.
O Cuckoo! shall I call thee Bird,
Or but a wandering Voice?

While I am lying on the grass
Thy twofold shout I hear,
From hill to hill it seems to pass,
At once far off, and near.

Though babbling only to the Vale,
Of sunshine and of flowers,
Thou bringest unto me a tale
Of visionary hours.

Thrice welcome, darling of the Spring!
Even yet thou art to me
No bird, but an invisible thing,
A voice, a mystery;

The same whom in my school-boy days
I listened to; that Cry
Which made me look a thousand ways
In bush, and tree, and sky.

To seek thee did I often rove
Through woods and on the green;
And thou wert still a hope, a love;
Still longed for, never seen.

And I can listen to thee yet;
Can lie upon the plain
And listen, till I do beget
That golden time again.

O blessed Bird! the earth we pace
Again appears to be
An unsubstantial, faery place;
That is fit home for Thee!

I Wandered Lonely as a Cloud

I wandered lonely as a cloud
That floats on high o'er vales and hills,
When all at once I saw a crowd,
A host, of golden daffodils;
Beside the lake, beneath the trees,
Fluttering and dancing in the breeze.

Continuous as the stars that shine
And twinkle on the milky way,
They stretched in never-ending line
Along the margin of a bay:
Ten thousand saw I at a glance,
Tossing their heads in sprightly dance.

The waves beside them danced; but they
Out-did the sparkling waves in glee:
A poet could not but be gay,
In such a jocund company:
I gazed—and gazed—but little thought
What wealth the show to me had brought:

For oft, when on my couch I lie
In vacant or in pensive mood,
They flash upon that inward eye
Which is the bliss of solitude;
And then my heart with pleasure fills,
And dances with the daffodils.

To the Supreme Being

The prayers I make will then be sweet indeed
If Thou the spirit give by which I pray:
My unassisted heart is barren clay,
That of its native self can nothing feed:
Of good and pious works thou art the seed,
That quickens only where thou say'st it may.
Unless Thou shew to us thine own true way
No man can find it: Father! Thou must lead.
Do Thou, then, breathe those thoughts into
    my mind
By which such virtue may in me be bred
That in thy holy footsteps I may tread;
The fetters of my tongue do Thou unbind,
That I may have the power to sing of thee,
And sound thy praises everlastingly.

To a Sky-Lark

Up with me! up with me into the clouds!
    For thy song, Lark, is strong;
Up with me, up with me into the clouds!
    Singing, singing,
With clouds and sky about thee ringing,
    Lift me, guide me till I find
That spot which seems so to thy mind!

I have walked through wildernesses dreary,
And to-day my heart is weary;
Had I now the wings of a Faery,
Up to thee would I fly.
There is madness about thee, and joy divine
In that song of thine;
Lift me, guide me high and high
To thy banqueting-place in the sky.

    Joyous as morning,
Thou art laughing and scorning;
Thou hast a nest for thy love and thy rest,
And, though little troubled with sloth,
Drunken Lark! thou would'st be loth
To be such a traveller as I.
Happy, happy Liver,
With a soul as strong as a mountain river
Pouring out praise to the almighty Giver,
    Joy and jollity be with us both!

Alas! my journey, rugged and uneven,
Through prickly moors or dusty ways must wind;
But hearing thee, or others of thy kind,
As full of gladness and as free of heaven,
I, with my fate contented, will plod on,
And hope for higher raptures, when life's day is done.

Louisa

I met Louisa in the shade,
And, having seen that lovely Maid,
Why should I fear to say
That, nymph-like, she is fleet and strong,
And down the rocks can leap along
Like rivulets in May?

She loves her fire, her cottage-home;
Yet o'er the moorland will she roam
In weather rough and bleak;
And, when against the wind she strains,
Oh! might I kiss the mountain rains
That sparkle on her cheek.

Take all that's mine "beneath the moon,"
If I with her but half a noon
May sit beneath the walls
Of some old cave, or mossy nook,
When up she winds along the brook
To hunt the waterfalls.

Admonition

Well may'st thou halt—and gaze with brightening
    eye!
The lovely Cottage in the guardian nook
Hath stirred thee deeply; with its own dear
    brook,
Its own small pasture, almost its own sky!
But covet not the Abode;—forbear to sigh,
As many do, repining while they look;
Intruders—who would tear from Nature's book
This precious leaf, with harsh impiety.
Think what the Home must be if it were thine,

Even thine, though few thy wants!—Roof, window,
  door,
The very flowers are sacred to the Poor,
The roses to the porch which they entwine:
Yea, all, that now enchants thee, from the day
On which it should be touched, would melt away.

"Beloved Vale!" I Said, "When I Shall Con"

"Beloved Vale!" I said, "when I shall con
Those many records of my childish years,
Remembrance of myself and of my peers
Will press me down: to think of what is gone
Will be an awful thought, if life have one."
But, when into the Vale I came, no fears
Distressed me; from mine eyes escaped no tears;
Deep thought, or dread remembrance, had I none.
By doubts and thousand petty fancies crost
I stood, of simple shame the blushing Thrall;
So narrow seemed the brooks, the fields so small!
A Juggler's balls old Time about him tossed;
I looked, I stared, I smiled, I laughed; and all
The weight of sadness was in wonder lost.

Composed by the Side of Grasmere Lake

Clouds, lingering yet, extend in solid bars
Through the grey west; and lo! these waters, steeled
By breezeless air to smoothest polish, yield
A vivid repetition of the stars;
Jove, Venus, and the ruddy crest of Mars
Amid his fellows beauteously revealed
At happy distance from earth's groaning field,
Where ruthless mortals wage incessant wars.

Is it a mirror?—or the nether Sphere
Opening to view the abyss in which she feeds
Her own calm fires?—But list! a voice is near;
Great Pan himself low-whispering through the reeds,
"Be thankful, thou; for, if unholy deeds
Ravage the world, tranquillity is here!"

With Ships the Sea was Sprinkled Far and Nigh

With Ships the sea was sprinkled far and nigh,
Like stars in heaven, and joyously it showed;
Some lying fast at anchor in the road,
Some veering up and down, one knew not why.
A goodly Vessel did I then espy
Come like a giant from a haven broad;
And lustily along the bay she strode,
Her tackling rich, and of apparel high.
This Ship was nought to me, nor I to her,
Yet I pursued her with a Lover's look;
This Ship to all the rest did I prefer:
When will she turn, and whither? She will brook
No tarrying; where She comes the winds must stir:
On went She, and due north her journey took.

Lines Composed at Grasmere During a Walk

Loud is the Vale! the Voice is up
With which she speaks when storms are gone,
A mighty Unison of streams!
Of all her Voices, One!

Loud is the Vale;—this inland Depth
In peace is roaring like the Sea;
Yon Star upon the mountain-top
Is listening quietly.

Sad was I, ev'n to pain depress'd,
Importunate and heavy load!
The Comforter hath found me here,
Upon this lonely road;

And many thousands now are sad,
Wait the fulfilment of their fear;
For He must die who is their Stay,
Their Glory disappear.

A Power is passing from the earth
To breathless Nature's dark abyss;
But when the Mighty pass away
What is it more than this,

That Man, who is from God sent forth,
Doth yet again to God return?—
Such ebb and flow must ever be,
Then wherefore should we mourn?

The Pass of Kirkstone

I

Within the mind strong fancies work,
A deep delight the bosom thrills,
Oft as I pass along the fork
Of these fraternal hills:
Where, save the rugged road, we find
No appanage of human kind,
Nor hint of man; if stone or rock
Seem not his handy-work to mock
By something cognizably shaped;
Mockery—or model roughly hewn,
And left as if by earthquake strewn,
Or from the Flood escaped:

Altars for Druid service fit;
(But where no fire was ever lit,
Unless the glow-worm to the skies
Thence offer nightly sacrifice)
Wrinkled Egyptian monument;
Green moss-grown tower; or hoary tent;
Tents of a camp that never shall be razed—
On which four thousand years have gazed!

II

Ye plough-shares sparkling on the slopes!
Ye snow-white lambs that trip
Imprisoned 'mid the formal props
Of restless ownership!
Ye trees, that may to-morrow fall
To feed the insatiate Prodigal!
Lawns, houses, chattels, groves, and fields,
All that the fertile valley shields;
Wages of folly—baits of crime,
Of life's uneasy game the stake,
Playthings that keep the eyes awake
Of drowsy, dotard Time;—
O care! O guilt!—O vales and plains,
Here, 'mid his own unvexed domains,
A Genius dwells, that can subdue
At once all memory of You,—
Most potent when mists veil the sky,
Mists that distort and magnify;
While the coarse rushes, to the sweeping breeze,
Sigh forth their ancient melodies!

III

List to those shriller notes!—*that* march
Perchance was on the blast,
When, through this Height's inverted arch,
Rome's earliest legion passed!
—They saw, adventurously impelled,
And older eyes than theirs beheld,
This block—and yon, whose church-like frame
Gives to this savage Pass its name.
Aspiring Road! that lov'st to hide
Thy daring in a vapoury bourn,
Not seldom may the hour return
When thou shalt be my guide:
And I (as all men may find cause,
When life is at a weary pause,
And they have panted up the hill
Of duty with reluctant will)
Be thankful, even though tired and faint,
For the rich bounties of constraint;
Whence oft invigorating transports flow
That choice lacked courage to bestow!

IV

My Soul was grateful for delight
That wore a threatening brow;
A veil is lifted—can she slight
The scene that opens now?
Though habitation none appear,
The greenness tells, man must be there;
The shelter—that the perspective
Is of the clime in which we live;
Where Toil pursues his daily round;
Where Pity sheds sweet tears—and Love,
In woodbine bower or birchen grove,

Inflicts his tender wound.
—Who comes not hither ne'er shall know
How beautiful the world below;
Nor can he guess how lightly leaps
The brook adown the rocky steeps,
Farewell, thou desolate Domain!
Hope, pointing to the cultured plain,
Carols like a shepherd-boy;
And who is she?—Can that be Joy!
Who, with a sunbeam for her guide,
Smoothly skims the meadows wide;
While Faith, from yonder opening cloud,
To hill and vale proclaims aloud,
"Whate'er the weak may dread, the wicked dare,
Thy lot, O Man, is good, thy portion fair!"

Composed Upon an Evening of Extraordinary Splendour and Beauty

I

Had this effulgence disappeared
With flying haste, I might have sent,
Among the speechless clouds, a look
Of blank astonishment;
But 'tis endued with power to stay,
And sanctify one closing day,
That frail Mortality may see—
What is?—ah no, but what *can* be!
Time was when field and watery cove
With modulated echoes rang,
While choirs of fervent Angels sang
Their vespers in the grove;
Or, crowning, star-like, each some sovereign height,

Warbled, for heaven above and earth below,
Strains, suitable to both.—Such holy rite,
Methinks, if audibly repeated now
From hill or valley, could not move
Sublimer transport, purer love,
Than doth this silent spectacle—the gleam—
The shadow—and the peace supreme!

II

No sound is uttered,—but a deep
And solemn harmony pervades
The hollow vale from steep to steep,
And penetrates the glades.
Far-distant images draw nigh,
Called forth by wondrous potency
Of beamy radiance, that imbues
Whate'er it strikes, with gem-like hues!
In vision exquisitely clear,
Herds range along the mountain side;
And glistening antlers are descried;
And gilded flocks appear.
Thine is the tranquil hour, purpureal Eve!
But long as god-like wish, or hope divine,
Informs my spirit, ne'er can I believe
That this magnificence is wholly thine!
—From worlds not quickened by the sun
A portion of the gift is won;
An intermingling of Heaven's pomp is spread
On ground which British shepherds tread!

III

And, if there be whom broken ties
Afflict, or injuries assail,
Yon hazy ridges to their eyes

Present a glorious scale,
Climbing suffused with sunny air,
To stop—no record hath told where!
And tempting Fancy to ascend,
And with immortal Spirits blend!
—Wings at my shoulders seem to play;
But, rooted here, I stand and gaze
On those bright steps that heaven-ward raise
Their practicable way.
Come forth, ye drooping old men, look abroad,
And see to what fair countries ye are bound!
And if some traveller, weary of his road,
Hath slept since noontide on the grassy ground,
Ye Genii! to his covert speed;
And wake him with such gentle heed
As may attune his soul to meet the dower
Bestowed on this transcendent hour!

IV

Such hues from their celestial Urn
Were wont to stream before mine eye,
Where'er it wandered in the morn
Of blissful infancy.
This glimpse of glory, why renewed?
Nay, rather speak with gratitude;
For, if a vestige of those gleams
Survived, 'twas only in my dreams.
Dread Power! whom peace and calmness serve
No less than Nature's threatening voice,
If aught unworthy be my choice,
From THEE if I would swerve;
Oh, let thy grace remind me of the light
Full early lost, and fruitlessly deplored;
Which, at this moment, on my waking sight

Appears to shine, by miracle restored;
My soul, though yet confined to earth,
Rejoices in a second birth!
—'Tis past, the visionary splendour fades;
And night approaches with her shades.

Gordale

At early dawn, or rather when the air
Glimmers with fading light, and shadowy Eve
Is busiest to confer and to bereave;
Then, pensive Votary! let thy feet repair
To Gordale-chasm, terrific as the lair
Where the young lions couch; for so, by leave
Of the propitious hour, thou may'st perceive
The local Deity, with oozy hair
And mineral crown, beside his jagged urn,
Recumbent: Him thou may'st behold, who hides
His lineaments by day, yet there presides,
Teaching the docile waters how to turn,
Or (if need be) impediment to spurn,
And force their passage to the salt-sea tides!

The Wild Duck's Nest

The imperial Consort of the Fairy-king
Owns not a sylvan bower; or gorgeous cell
With emerald floored, and with purpureal shell
Ceilinged and roofed; that is so fair a thing
As this low structure, for the tasks of Spring,
Prepared by one who loves the buoyant swell
Of the brisk waves, yet here consents to dwell;
And spreads in steadfast peace her brooding
    wing.

Words cannot paint the o'ershadowing yew-tree
   bough,
And dimly-gleaming Nest,—a hollow crown
Of golden leaves inlaid with silver down,
Fine as the mother's softest plumes allow:
I gazed—and, self-accused while gazing, sighed
For human-kind, weak slaves of cumbrous pride!

To a Snow-Drop

Lone Flower, hemmed in with snows and white as
   they
But hardier far, once more I see thee bend
Thy forehead, as if fearful to offend,
Like an unbidden guest. Though day by day,
Storms, sallying from the mountain-tops, way-lay
The rising sun, and on the plains descend;
Yet art thou welcome, welcome as a friend
Whose zeal outruns his promise! Blue-eyed May
Shall soon behold this border thickly set
With bright jonquils, their odours lavishing
On the soft west-wind and his frolic peers;
Nor will I then thy modest grace forget,
Chaste Snow-drop, venturous harbinger of Spring,
And pensive monitor of fleeting years!

There is a Little Unpretending Rill

There is a little unpretending Rill
Of limpid water, humbler far than aught
That ever among Men or Naiads sought
Notice or name!—It quivers down the hill,
Furrowing its shallow way with dubious will;
Yet to my mind this scanty Stream is brought

Oftener than Ganges or the Nile; a thought
Of private recollection sweet and still!
Months perish with their moons; year treads on year;
But, faithful Emma! thou with me canst say
That, while ten thousand pleasures disappear,
And flies their memory fast almost as they,
The immortal Spirit of one happy day
Lingers beside that Rill, in vision clear.

The Stars Are Mansions Built By Nature's Hand

The stars are mansions built by Nature's hand,
And, haply, there the spirits of the blest
Dwell, clothed in radiance, their immortal vest;
Huge Ocean shows, within his yellow strand,
A habitation marvellously planned,
For life to occupy in love and rest;
All that we see—is dome, or vault, or nest,
Or fortress, reared at Nature's sage command.
Glad thought for every season! but the Spring
Gave it while cares were weighing on my heart,
'Mid song of birds, and insects murmuring;
And while the youthful year's prolific art—
Of bud, leaf, blade, and flower—was fashioning
Abodes where self-disturbance hath no part.

Sole Listener, Duddon! To the Breeze that Played

Sole listener, Duddon! to the breeze that played
With thy clear voice, I caught the fitful sound
Wafted o'er sullen moss and craggy mound—
Unfruitful solitudes, that seemed to upbraid
The sun in heaven!—but now, to form a shade
For Thee, green alders have together wound

Their foliage; ashes flung their arms around;
And birch-trees risen in silver colonnade.
And thou hast also tempted here to rise,
'Mid sheltering pines, this Cottage rude and grey;
Whose ruddy children, by the mother's eyes
Carelessly watched, sport through the summer day,
Thy pleased associates:—light as endless May
On infant bosoms lonely Nature lies.

Who Swerves From Innocence, Who Makes Divorce

Who swerves from innocence, who makes divorce
Of that serene companion—a good name,
Recovers not his loss; but walks with shame,
With doubt, with fear, and haply with remorse:
And oft-times he—who, yielding to the force
Of chance-temptation, ere his journey end,
From chosen comrade turns, or faithful friend—
In vain shall rue the broken intercourse.
Not so with such as loosely wear the chain
That binds them, pleasant River! to thy side:—
Through the rough copse wheel thou with hasty
      stride;
I choose to saunter o'er the grassy plain,
Sure, when the separation has been tried,
That we, who part in love, shall meet again.

Conclusion (of the Duddon Sonnets)

But here no cannon thunders to the gale;
Upon the wave no haughty pendants cast
A crimson splendour: lowly is the mast
That rises here, and humbly spread, the sail;
While, less disturbed than in the narrow Vale

Through which with strange vicissitudes he passed,
The Wanderer seeks that receptacle vast
Where all his unambitious functions fail.
And may thy Poet, cloud-born Stream! be free—
The sweets of earth contentedly resigned,
And each tumultuous working left behind
At seemly distance—to advance like Thee;
Prepared, in peace of heart, in calm of mind
And soul, to mingle with Eternity!

Thought on the Seasons

FLATTERED with promise of escape
    From every hurtful blast,
Spring takes, O sprightly May! thy shape,
    Her loveliest and her last.

Less fair is summer riding high
    In fierce solstitial power,
Less fair than when a lenient sky
    Brings on her parting hour.

When earth repays with golden sheaves
    The labours of the plough,
And ripening fruits and forest leaves
    All brighten on the bough;

What pensive beauty autumn shows,
    Before she hears the sound
Of winter rushing in, to close
    The emblematic round!

Such be our Spring, our Summer such;
    So may our Autumn blend
With hoary Winter, and Life touch,
    Through heaven-born hope, her end!

The Brownie

"How disappeared he?" Ask the newt and toad;
Ask of his fellow men, and they will tell
How he was found, cold as an icicle,
Under an arch of that forlorn abode;
Where he, unpropp'd, and by the gathering flood
Of years hemm'd round, had dwelt, prepared to try
Privation's worst extremities, and die
With no one near save the omnipresent God.
Verily so to live was an awful choice—
A choice that wears the aspect of a doom;
But in the mould of mercy all is cast
For Souls familiar with the eternal Voice;
And this forgotten Taper to the last
Drove from itself, we trust, all frightful gloom.

To the Planet Venus, an Evening Star

Composed at Loch Lomond

Though joy attend Thee orient at the birth
Of dawn, it cheers the lofty spirit most
To watch thy course when Day-light, fled from earth,
In the grey sky hath left his lingering Ghost,
Perplexed as if between a splendour lost
And splendour slowly mustering. Since the Sun,
The absolute, the world-absorbing One,
Relinquished half his empire to the host
Emboldened by thy guidance, holy Star,
Holy as princely, who that looks on thee
Touching, as now, in thy humility
The mountain borders of this seat of care,
Can question that thy countenance is bright,
Celestial Power, as much with love as light?

Calm is the Fragrant Air, and Loth to Lose

Calm is the fragrant air, and loth to lose
Day's grateful warmth, tho' moist with falling dews.
Look for the stars, you'll say that there are none;
Look up a second time, and, one by one,
You mark them twinkling out with silvery light,
And wonder how they could elude the sight!
The birds, of late so noisy in their bowers,
Warbled a while with faint and fainter powers,
But now are silent as the dim-seen flowers:
Nor does the village Church-clock's iron tone
The time's and season's influence disown;
Nine beats distinctly to each other bound
In drowsy sequence—how unlike the sound
That, in rough winter, oft inflicts a fear
On fireside listeners, doubting what they hear!
The shepherd, bent on rising with the sun,
Had closed his door before the day was done,
And now with thankful heart to bed doth creep,
And joins his little children in their sleep.
The bat, lured forth where trees the lane o'ershade,
Flits and reflits along the close arcade;
The busy dor-hawk chases the white moth
With burring note, which Industry and Sloth
Might both be pleased with, for it suits them both.
A stream is heard—I see it not, but know
By its soft music whence the waters flow:
Wheels and the tread of hoofs are heard no more;
One boat there was, but it will touch the shore
With the next dipping of its slackened oar;
Faint sound, that, for the gayest of the gay,
Might give to serious thought a moment's sway,
As a last token of man's toilsome day!

Rural Illusions

Sylph was it? or a Bird more bright
    Than those of fabulous stock?
A second darted by;—and lo!
    Another of the flock,
Through sunshine flitting from the bough
    To nestle in the rock.
Transient deception! a gay freak
    Of April's mimicries!
Those brilliant strangers, hailed with joy
    Among the budding trees,
Proved last year's leaves, pushed from the spray
    To frolic on the breeze.

Maternal Flora! show thy face,
    And let thy hand be seen,
Thy hand here sprinkling tiny flowers,
    That, as they touch the green,
Take root (so seems it) and look up
    In honour of their Queen.
Yet, sooth, those little starry specks,
    That not in vain aspired
To be confounded with live growths,
    Most dainty, most admired,
Were only blossoms dropped from twigs
    Of their own offspring tired.

Not such the World's illusive shows;
    Her wingless flutterings,
Her blossoms which, though shed, outbrave
    The floweret as it springs,
For the undeceived, smile as they may,
    Are melancholy things:
But gentle Nature plays her part
    With ever-varying wiles,

And transient feignings with plain truth
    So well she reconciles,
That those fond Idlers most are pleased
    Whom oftenest she beguiles.

A Wren's Nest

Among the dwellings framed by birds
    In field or forest with nice care,
Is none that with the little Wren's
    In snugness may compare.

No door the tenement requires,
    And seldom needs a laboured roof;
Yet is it to the fiercest sun
    Impervious, and storm-proof.

So warm, so beautiful withal,
    In perfect fitness for its aim,
That to the Kind by special grace
    Their instinct surely came.

And when for their abodes they seek
    An opportune recess,
The hermit has no finer eye
    For shadowy quietness.

These find, 'mid ivied abbey-walls,
    A canopy in some still nook;
Others are pent-housed by a brae
    That overhangs a brook.

There to the brooding bird her mate
    Warbles by fits his low clear song;
And by the busy streamlet both
    Are sung to all day long.

Or in sequestered lanes they build,
    Where, till the flitting bird's return,
Her eggs within the nest repose,
    Like relics in an urn.

But still, where general choice is good,
    There is a better and a best;
And, among fairest objects, some
    Are fairer than the rest;

This, one of those small builders proved
    In a green covert, where, from out
The forehead of a pollard oak,
    The leafy antlers sprout;

For She who planned the mossy lodge,
    Mistrusting her evasive skill,
Had to a Primrose looked for aid
    Her wishes to fulfil.

High on the trunk's projecting brow
    And fixed an infant's span above
The budding flowers, peeped forth the nest,
    The prettiest of the grove!

The treasure proudly did I show
    To some whose minds without disdain
Can turn to little things; but once
    Looked up for it in vain:

'Tis gone—a ruthless spoiler's prey,
    Who heeds not beauty, love, or song,
'Tis gone! (so seemed it) and we grieved
    Indignant at the wrong.

Just three days after, passing by
    In clearer light the moss-built cell
I saw, espied its shaded mouth;
    And felt that all was well.

The Primrose for a veil had spread
    The largest of her upright leaves;
And thus, for purposes benign,
    A simple flower deceives.

Concealed from friends who might disturb
    Thy quiet with no ill intent,
Secure from evil eyes and hands
    On barbarous plunder bent,

Rest, Mother-bird! and when thy young
    Take flight, and thou art free to roam,
When withered is the guardian Flower,
    And empty thy late home,

Think how ye prospered, thou and thine,
    Amid the unviolated grove
Housed near the growing Primrose-tuft
    In foresight, or in love.

On a High Part of the Coast of Cumberland

The Sun, that seemed so mildly to retire,
Flung back from distant climes a streaming fire,
Whose blaze is now subdued to tender gleams,
Prelude of night's approach with soothing
    dreams.
Look round;—of all the clouds not one is moving;
'Tis the still hour of thinking, feeling, loving.
Silent, and stedfast as the vaulted sky,
The boundless plain of waters seems to lie:—
Comes that low sound from breezes rustling o'er
The grass-crowned headland that conceals the shore?
No; 'tis the earth-voice of the mighty sea,
Whispering how meek and gentle he *can* be!

Thou Power supreme! who, arming to rebuke
Offenders, dost put off the gracious look,
And clothe thyself with terrors like the flood
Of ocean roused into his fiercest mood,
Whatever discipline thy Will ordain
For the brief course that must for me remain;
Teach me with quick-eared spirit to rejoice
In admonitions of thy softest voice!
Whate'er the path these mortal feet may trace,
Breathe through my soul the blessing of thy grace,
Glad, through a perfect love, a faith sincere
Drawn from the wisdom that begins with fear,
Glad to expand; and, for a season, free
From finite cares, to rest absorbed in Thee!

Why Should the Enthusiast, Journeying Through this Isle

Why should the Enthusiast, journeying through this
    Isle,
Repine as if his hour were come too late?
Not unprotected in her mouldering state,
Antiquity salutes him with a smile,
'Mid fruitful fields that ring with jocund toil,
And pleasure-grounds where Taste, refined
    Co-mate
Of Truth and Beauty, strives to imitate,
Far as she may, primeval Nature's style.
Fair Land! by Time's parental love made free,
By Social Order's watchful arms embraced;
With unexampled union meet in thee,
For eye and mind, the present and the past;
With golden prospect for futurity,
If that be reverenced which ought to last.

By the Sea-Shore, Isle of Man

Why stand we gazing on the sparkling Brine,
With wonder smit by its transparency,
And all-enraptured with its purity?—
Because the unstained, the clear, the crystalline,
Have ever in them something of benign;
Whether in gem, in water, or in sky,
A sleeping infant's brow, or wakeful eye
Of a young maiden, only not divine.
Scarcely the hand forbears to dip its palm
For beverage drawn as from a mountain-well.
Temptation centres in the liquid Calm;
Our daily raiment seems no obstacle
To instantaneous plunging in, deep Sea!
And revelling in long embrace with thee.

Most Sweet it is with Unuplifted Eyes

Most sweet it is with unuplifted eyes
To pace the ground, if path be there or none,
While a fair region round the traveller lies
Which he forbears again to look upon;
Pleased rather with some soft ideal scene,
The work of Fancy, or some happy tone
Of meditation, slipping in between
The beauty coming and the beauty gone.
If Thought and Love desert us, from that day
Let us break off all commerce with the Muse:
With Thought and Love companions of our way,
Whate'er the senses take or may refuse,
The Mind's internal heaven shall shed her dews
Of inspiration on the humblest lay.

Not in the Lucid Intervals of Life

Not in the lucid intervals of life
That come but as a curse to party-strife;
Not in some hour when Pleasure with a sigh
Of languor puts his rosy garland by;
Not in the breathing-times of that poor slave
Who daily piles up wealth in Mammon's cave—
Is Nature felt, or can be; nor do words,
Which practised talent readily affords,
Prove that her hand has touched responsive chords;
Nor has her gentle beauty power to move
With genuine rapture and with fervent love
The soul of Genius, if he dare to take
Life's rule from passion craved for passion's sake;
Untaught that meekness is the cherished bent
Of all the truly great and all the innocent.

But who *is* innocent? By grace divine,
Not otherwise, O Nature! we are thine,
Through good and evil thine, in just degree
Of rational and manly sympathy.
To all that Earth from pensive hearts is stealing,
And Heaven is now to gladdened eyes revealing,
Add every charm the Universe can show
Through every change its aspects undergo—
Care may be respited, but not repealed;
No perfect cure grows on that bounded field.
Vain is the pleasure, a false calm the peace,
If He, through whom alone our conflicts cease,
Our virtuous hopes without relapse advance,
Come not to speed the Soul's deliverance;
To the distempered Intellect refuse
His gracious help, or give what we abuse.

By the Side of Rydal Mere

The linnet's warble, sinking towards a close,
Hints to the thrush 'tis time for their repose;
The shrill-voiced thrush is heedless, and again
The monitor revives his own sweet strain;
But both will soon be mastered, and the copse
Be left as silent as the mountain-tops,
Ere some commanding star dismiss to rest
The throng of rooks, that now, from twig or nest,
(After a steady flight on home-bound wings,
And a last game of mazy hoverings
Around their ancient grove) with cawing noise
Disturb the liquid music's equipoise.

O Nightingale! Who ever heard thy song
Might here be moved, till Fancy grows so strong
That listening sense is pardonably cheated
Where wood or stream by thee was never
    greeted.
Surely, from fairest spots of favoured lands,
Were not some gifts withheld by jealous hands,
This hour of deepening darkness here would be
As a fresh morning for new harmony;
And lays as prompt would hail the dawn of
    Night:
A dawn she has both beautiful and bright,
When the East kindles with the full moon's light;
Not like the rising sun's impatient glow
Dazzling the mountains, but an overflow
Of solemn splendour, in mutation slow.

Wanderer by spring with gradual progress led,
For sway profoundly felt as widely spread;
To king, to peasant, to rough sailor, dear,
And to the soldier's trumpet-wearied ear;

How welcome wouldst thou be to this green
    Vale
Fairer than Tempe! Yet, sweet Nightingale!
From the warm breeze that bears thee on, alight
At will, and stay thy migratory flight;
Build, at thy choice, or sing, by pool or fount,
Who shall complain, or call thee to account?
The wisest, happiest, of our kind are they
That ever walk content with Nature's way,
God's goodness—measuring bounty as it may;
For whom the gravest thought of what they miss,
Chastening the fulness of a present bliss,
Is with that wholesome office satisfied,
While unrepining sadness is allied
In thankful bosoms to a modest pride.

Ode Composed on May Morning

While from the purpling east departs
    The star that led the dawn,
Blithe Flora from her couch upstarts,
    For May is on the lawn,
A quickening hope, a freshening glee,
    Foreran the expected Power,
Whose first-drawn breath, from bush and tree,
    Shakes off that pearly shower.

All Nature welcomes Her whose sway
    Tempers the year's extremes;
Who scattereth lustres o'er noon-day,
    Like morning's dewy gleams;
While mellow warble, sprightly trill,
    The tremulous heart excite;
And hums the balmy air to still
    The balance of delight.

Time was, blest Power! when youths and maids
    At peep of dawn would rise,
And wander forth in forest glades
    Thy birth to solemnize.
Though mute the song—to grace the rite
    Untouched the hawthorn bough,
Thy Spirit triumphs o'er the slight;
    Man changes, but not Thou!

Thy feathered Lieges bill and wings
    In love's disport employ;
Warmed by thy influence, creeping things
    Awake to silent joy:
Queen art thou still for each gay plant
    Where the slim wild deer roves;
And served in depths where fishes haunt
    Their own mysterious groves.

Cloud-piercing peak, and trackless heath,
    Instinctive homage pay;
Nor wants the dim-lit cave a wreath
    To honour thee, sweet May!
Where cities fanned by thy brisk airs
    Behold a smokeless sky,
Their puniest flower-pot-nursling dares
    To open a bright eye.

And if, on this thy natal morn,
    The pole, from which thy name
Hath not departed, stands forlorn
    Of song and dance and game;
Still from the village-green a vow
    Aspires to thee addrest,
Wherever peace is on the brow,
    Or love within the breast.

Yes! where Love nestles thou canst teach
    The soul to love the more;
Hearts also shall thy lessons reach
    That never loved before.
Stript is the haughty one of pride,
    The bashful freed from fear,
While rising, like the ocean-tide,
    In flows the joyous year.

Hush, feeble lyre! weak words refuse
    The service to prolong!
To yon exulting thrush the Muse
    Entrusts the imperfect song;
His voice shall chant, in accents clear,
    Throughout the live-long day,
Till the first silver star appear,
    The sovereignty of May.

Airey-Force Valley

————Not a breath of air
Ruffles the bosom of this leafy glen.
From the brook's margin, wide around, the
    trees
Are stedfast as the rocks; the brook itself,
Old as the hills that feed it from afar,
Doth rather deepen than disturb the calm
Where all things else are still and motionless.
And yet, even now, a little breeze, perchance
Escaped from boisterous winds that rage
    without,
Has entered, by the sturdy oaks unfelt,
But to its gentle touch how sensitive
Is the light ash! that, pendent from the brow

Of yon dim cave, in seeming silence makes
A soft eye-music of slow-waving boughs,
Powerful almost as vocal harmony
To stay the wanderer's steps and soothe his thoughts.

To the Clouds

Army of Clouds! ye winged Hosts in troops
Ascending from behind the motionless brow
Of that tall rock, as from a hidden world,
Oh whither with such eagerness of speed?
What seek ye, or what shun ye? of the gale
Companions, fear ye to be left behind,
Or racing o'er your blue ethereal field
Contend ye with each other? of the sea
Children, thus post ye over vale and height
  To sink upon your's mother's lap—and rest?
Or were ye rightlier hailed, when first mine eyes
Beheld in your impetuous march the likeness
Of a wide army pressing on to meet
Or overtake some unknown enemy?—
But your smooth motions suit a peaceful aim;
And Fancy, not less aptly pleased, compares
Your squadrons to an endless flight of birds
Aerial, upon due migration bound
To milder climes; or rather do ye urge
In caravan your hasty pilgrimage
To pause at last on more aspiring heights
Than these, and utter your devotion there
With thunderous voice? Or are ye jubilant,
And would ye, tracking your proud lord the Sun,
Be present at his setting; or the pomp
Of Persian mornings would ye fill, and stand
Poising your splendours high above the heads

Of worshippers kneeling to their up-risen God?
Whence, whence, ye Clouds! this eagerness of speed?
Speak, silent creatures.—They are gone, are fled,
Buried together in yon gloomy mass
That loads the middle heaven; and clear and bright
And vacant doth the region which they thronged
Appear; a calm descent of sky conducting
Down to the unapproachable abyss,
Down to that hidden gulf from which they rose
To vanish—fleet as days and months and years,
Fleet as the generations of mankind,
Power, glory, empire, as the world itself,
The lingering world, when time hath ceased to be.
But the winds roar, shaking the rooted trees,
And see! a bright precursor to a train
Perchance as numerous, overpeers the rock
That sullenly refuses to partake
Of the wild impulse. From a fount of life
Invisible, the long procession moves
Luminous or gloomy, welcome to the vale
Which they are entering, welcome to mine eye
That sees them, to my soul that owns in them,
And in the bosom of the firmament
O'er which they move, wherein they are contained,
A type of her capacious self and all
Her restless progeny.
    A humble walk
Here is my body doomed to tread, this path,
A little hoary line and faintly traced,
Work, shall we call it, of the shepherd's foot
Or of his flock?—joint vestige of them both.
I pace it unrepining, for my thoughts
Admit no bondage and my words have wings.
Where is the Orphean lyre, or Druid harp,

To accompany the verse? The mountain blast
Shall be our 'hand' of music; he shall sweep
The rocks, and quivering trees, and billowy lake,
And search the fibres of the caves, and they
Shall answer, for our song is of the Clouds
And the wind loves them; and the gentle gales—
Which by their aid re-clothe the naked lawn
With annual verdure, and revive the woods,
And moisten the parched lips of thirsty
    flowers—
Love them; and every idle breeze of air
Bends to the favourite burthen. Moon and stars
Keep their most solemn vigils when the Clouds
Watch also, shifting peaceably their place
Like bands of ministering Spirits, or when
    they lie,
As if some Protean art the change had wrought,
In listless quiet o'er the ethereal deep
Scattered, a Cyclades of various shapes
And all degrees of beauty. O ye Lightnings!
Ye are their perilous offspring; and the Sun—
Source inexhaustible of life and joy,
And type of man's far-darting reason, therefore
In old time worshipped as the god of verse,
A blazing intellectual deity—
Loves his own glory in their looks, and showers
Upon that unsubstantial brotherhood
Visions with all but beatific light
Enriched—too transient were they not renewed
From age to age, and did not, while we gaze
In silent rapture, credulous desire
Nourish the hope that memory lacks not power
To keep the treasure unimpaired. Vain thought!
Yet why repine, created as we are

For joy and rest, albeit to find them only
Lodged in the bosom of eternal things?

On the Projected Kendal and Windermere Railway

Is then no nook of English ground secure
From rash assault? Schemes of retirement sown
In youth, and 'mid the busy world kept pure
As when their earliest flowers of hope were blown,
Must perish;—how can they this blight endure?
And must he too the ruthless change bemoan
Who scorns a false utilitarian lure
'Mid his paternal fields at random thrown?
Baffle the threat, bright Scene, from Orresthead
Given to the pausing traveller's rapturous glance:
Plead for thy peace, thou beautiful romance
Of nature; and, if human hearts be dead,
Speak, passing winds; ye torrents, with your strong
And constant voice, protest against the wrong.

Glad Sight Wherever New With Old

Glad sight wherever new with old
Is joined through some dear homeborn tie;
The life of all that we behold
Depends upon that mystery.
Vain is the glory of the sky,
The beauty vain of field and grove,
Unless, while with admiring eye
We gaze, we also learn to love.

So Fair, so Sweet, Withal so Sensitive

SO fair, so sweet, withal so sensitive,
Would that the little Flowers were born to live,
Conscious of half the pleasure which they give;

That to this mountain-daisy's self were known
The beauty of its star-shaped shadow, thrown
On the smooth surface of this naked stone!

And what if hence a bold desire should mount
High as the Sun, that he could take account
Of all that issues from his glorious fount!

So might he ken how by his sovereign aid
These delicate companionships are made;
And how he rules the pomp of light and shade;

And were the Sister-power that shines by night
So privileged, what a countenance of delight
Would through the clouds break forth on human
   sight!

Fond fancies! wheresoe'er shall turn thine eye
On earth, air, ocean, or the starry sky,
Converse with Nature in pure sympathy;

All vain desires, all lawless wishes quelled,
Be Thou to love and praise alike impelled,
Whatever boon is granted or withheld.